BRITISH RAILV

CO

STOCK

TWENTY-SIXTH EDITION
2002

The complete guide to all Locomotive-Hauled Coaches which operate on the Railtrack network

Peter Fox & Peter Hall

PLATFORM 5

ISBN 1 902336 22 4

CONTENTS

PROVISION OF INFORMATION

This book has been compiled with care to be as accurate as possible, but in some cases official information is not available and the publisher cannot be held responsible for any errors or omissions. We would like to thank the companies and individuals which have been co-operative in supplying information to us. The authors of this series of books will be pleased to receive notification from readers of any inaccuracies readers may find in the series, and also notification of any additional information to supplement our records and thus enhance future editions. Please send comments to:

Peter Hall, 4 Ladies Spring Court, Ladies Spring Grove, Dore, Sheffield, S17 3LR.
Tel: 0114 262 0693 Fax: 0114 236 5693.
e-mail: peter@hall59.freeserve.co.uk

Both the author and the staff of Platform 5 regret they are unable to answer specific queries regarding locomotives and rolling stock.

This book is updated to 29 October 2001.

UPDATES

An update to all the books in the *British Railways Pocket Book* series is published every month in the new Platform 5 magazine, **entrain**, which contains news and rolling stock information on the railways of Britain and Ireland . For further details of entrain, please see the advertisement inside the front cover of this book.

BRITAIN'S RAILWAY SYSTEM

INFRASTRUCTURE & OPERATION

Britain's national railway infrastructure is owned by a public company – Railtrack PLC (now in administration). Many stations and maintenance depots are leased to and operated by Train Operating Companies (TOCs), but some larger stations remain under Railtrack control. The only exception is the infrastructure on the Isle of Wight, which is nationally owned and is leased to the Island Line franchisee.

Trains are operated by TOCs over the Railtrack network, regulated by access agreements between the parties involved. In general, TOCs are responsible for the provision and maintenance of the locomotives, rolling stock and staff necessary for the direct operation of services, whilst Railtrack is responsible for the provision and maintenance of the infrastructure and also for staff needed to regulate the operation of services.

DOMESTIC PASSENGER TRAIN OPERATORS

The large majority of passenger trains are operated by the TOCs on fixed term franchises. Franchise expiry dates are shown in parentheses in the list of franchisees below:

Franchise	*Franchisee*	*Trading Name*
Anglia Railways	GB Railways Ltd. (until 4 April 2004)	Anglia Railways
Central Trains	National Express Group PLC (until 1 April 2004)	Central Trains
Chiltern Railways	M40 Trains Ltd. (until 20 July 2003)	Chiltern Railways
Cross Country	Virgin Rail Group Ltd. (until 4 January 2012)	Virgin Trains
Gatwick Express	National Express Group PLC (until 27 April 2011)	Gatwick Express
Great Eastern Railway	First Group PLC (until 4 April 2004)	First Great Eastern
Great Western Trains	First Group PLC (until 3 February 2006)	First Great Western
InterCity East Coast	GNER Holdings Ltd. (until 4 April 2004)	Great North Eastern Railway
InterCity West Coast	Virgin Rail Group Ltd. (until 8 March 2012)	Virgin Trains
Island Line	Stagecoach Holdings PLC (until 12 October 2003)	Island Line
LTS Rail	National Express Group PLC (until 25 May 2011)	c2c
Merseyrail Electrics	Arriva PLC (until 18 February 2003)	Arriva Trains Merseyside
Midland Main Line	National Express Group PLC (until 27 April 2008)	Midland Mainline

North London Railways	National Express Group PLC (until 1 September 2004)	Silverlink Train Services
North West Regional Railways	First Group PLC (until 1 April 2004)	First North Western
Regional Railways North East	Arriva PLC (until 18 February 2003)	Arriva Trains Northern
Scotrail	National Express Group PLC (until 30 March 2004)	ScotRail
South Central	GoVia Ltd. (until 25 May 2003) §	South Central
South Eastern	Connex Transport UK Ltd. (until 12 October 2011)	Connex
South West	Stagecoach Holdings PLC (until 3 February 2023)	South West Trains
Thames	Victory Railways Holdings Ltd. (until 12 April 2004)	Thames Trains
Thameslink	GoVia Ltd. (until 1 April 2004)	Thameslink Rail
Great Northern	National Express Group PLC (until 31 May 2001)	WAGN
Wales & Borders*	National Express Group PLC (until 30 April 2004)	Wales & Borders Trains
Wessex Trains*	National Express Group PLC (until 30 April 2004)	Wessex Trains
West Anglia	National Express Group PLC (until 4 April 2004)	WAGN

Notes: * For the present, the existing Wales & West TOC is the legal trading name of Wessex Trains and the Cardiff Railway Company is the legal name for Wales & Borders pending the award of the new Wales & West and Wessex franchises.
§ Pending finalisation of new 20-year franchise.

The following operators run non-franchised services only:

Operator	*Trading Name*	*Route*
British Airports Authority	Heathrow Express	London Paddington–Heathrow Airport
Hull Trains	Hull Trains	London King's Cross–Hull
West Coast Railway Co.	West Coast Railway	Fort William–Mallaig

INTERNATIONAL PASSENGER OPERATIONS

Eurostar (UK) operates international passenger-only services between the United Kingdom and continental Europe, jointly with French National Railways (SNCF) and Belgian National Railways (SNCB/NMBS). Eurostar (UK) is a subsidiary of London & Continental Railways, which is jointly owned by National Express Group PLC and British Airways.

In addition, a service for the conveyance of accompanied road vehicles through the Channel Tunnel is provided by the tunnel operating company, Eurotunnel.

FREIGHT TRAIN OPERATIONS

Freight train services are operated under 'Open Access' arrangements by English Welsh & Scottish Railway (EWS), Freightliner, GB Railfreight Ltd. and Direct Rail Services .

INTRODUCTION

LAYOUT OF INFORMATION

Coaches are listed in numerical order of painted number in batches according to type.

Each coach entry is laid out as in the following example (former number column may be omitted where not applicable):

No.	*Prev. No.*	*Notes*	*Livery*	*Owner*	*Operation*	*Depot/Location*
3521	(3271)		**AR**	H	*AR*	NC

DETAILED INFORMATION & CODES

Under each type heading, the following details are shown:

- Diagram Code. This consists of the first three characters of the TOPS type code followed by two numbers which relate to the particular design of vehicle.
- 'Mark' of coach (see below).
- Descriptive text.
- Number of first class seats , standard class seats, lavatory compartments and wheelchair spaces shown as F/S nT nW respectively.
- Bogie type (see below).
- Additional features.
- ETH Index.

TOPS TYPE CODES

TOPS type codes are allocated to all coaching stock. For vehicles numbered in the passenger stock number series the code consists of:

(1) Two letters denoting the layout of the vehicle as follows:

AA Gangwayed Corridor
AB Gangwayed Corridor Brake
AC Gangwayed Open (2+2 seating)
AD Gangwayed Open (2+1 seating)
AE Gangwayed Open Brake
AF Gangwayed Driving Open Brake
AG Micro-Buffet
AH Brake Micro-Buffet
AI As 'AC' but with drop-head buckeye and gangway at one end only
AJ Restaurant Buffet with Kitchen

AK Kitchen Car
AL As 'AC' but with disabled person's toilet (Mark 4 only)
AN Miniature Buffet
AP Pullman First with Kitchen
AQ Pullman Parlour First
AR Pullman Brake First
AS Sleeping Car
AT Royal Train Coach
AU Sleeping Car with Pantry
AX Generator Van (1000 V d.c.)
AZ Special Saloon
GF DMU/EMU/Mark 4 Barrier Vehicle
AX Generator Van (415 V a.c three-phase)
NM Sandite Coach

(2) A digit denoting the class of passenger accommodation:

1	First	4	Unclassified
2	Standard (formerly second)	5	None
3	Composite (first & standard)		

(3) A suffix relating to the build of coach.

1	Mark 1	C	Mark 2C	G	Mark 3 or 3A
Z	Mark 2	D	Mark 2D	H	Mark 3B
A	Mark 2A	E	Mark 2E	J	Mark 4
B	Mark 2B	F	Mark 2F		

OPERATING CODES

Operating codes used by train company operating staff (and others) to denote vehicle types in general. These are shown in parentheses adjacent to TOPS type codes. Letters used are:

B	Brake	K	Side corridor with lavatory
C	Composite	O	Open
F	First Class	S	Standard Class (formerly second)

Various other letters are in use and the meaning of these can be ascertained by referring to the titles at the head of each type.

Readers should note the distinction between an SO (Open Standard) and a TSO (Tourist Open Standard) The former has 2+1 seating layout, whilst the latter has 2+2.

BOGIE TYPES

BR Mark 1 (BR1). Double bolster leaf spring bogie. Generally 90 m.p.h., but BR1 bogies may be permitted to run at 100 m.p.h. with special maintenance. Weight: 6.1 t.

BR Mark 2 (BR2). Single bolster leaf-spring bogie used on certain types of non-passenger stock and suburban stock (all now withdrawn). Weight: 5.3 t.

COMMONWEALTH (C). Heavy, cast steel coil spring bogie. 100 m.p.h. Weight: 6.75 t.

B4. Coil spring fabricated bogie. Generally 100 m.p.h., but B4 bogies may be permitted to run at 110 m.p.h. with special maintenance. Weight: 5.2 t.

B5. Heavy duty version of B4. 100 m.p.h. Weight: 5.3 t.

B5 (SR). A bogie originally used on Southern Region EMUs, similar in design to B5. Now also used on locomotive hauled coaches. 100 m.p.h.

BT10. A fabricated bogie designed for 125 m.p.h. Air suspension.

T4. A 125 m.p.h. bogie designed by BREL (now Bombardier Transportation).

BT41. Fitted to Mark 4 vehicles, designed by SIG in Switzerland. At present limited to 125 m.p.h., but designed for 140 m.p.h.

BRAKES

Air braking is now standard on British main line trains. Vehicles with other equipment are denoted:

v Vacuum braked.
x Dual braked (air and vacuum).

HEATING & VENTILATION

Electric heating and ventilation is now standard on British main-line trains. Certain coaches for use on charter services may in addition also have steam heating facilities, or be steam heated only.

PUBLIC ADDRESS

It is assumed all coaches are now fitted with public address equipment, although certain stored vehicles may not have this feature. In addition, it is assumed all vehicles with a conductor's compartment have public address transmission facilities, as have catering vehicles.

COOKING EQUIPMENT

It is assumed that Mark 1 catering vehicles have gas powered cooking equipment, whilst Mark 2, 3 and 4 catering vehicles have electric powered cooking equipment unless stated otherwise.

ADDITIONAL FEATURE CODES

d	Secondary door locking.
dg	Driver–Guard communication equipment.
f	Facelifted or fluorescent lighting.
k	Composition brake blocks (instead of cast iron).
n	Day/night lighting.
p	Public telephone.
pg	Public address transmission and driver-guard communication.
pt	Public address transmission facility.
q	Catering staff to shore telephone.
w	Wheelchair space.

z Disabled persons' toilet.

Standard class coaches with wheelchair space also have one tip-up seat per space.

NOTES ON ETH INDICES

The sum of ETH indices in a train must not be more than the ETS index of the locomotive. The normal voltage on British trains is 1000 V. Suffix 'X' denotes 600 amp wiring instead of 400 amp. Trains whose ETH index is higher than 66 must be formed completely of 600 amp wired stock. Class 33 locomotives cannot provide a consistent electric train supply for Mark 2D, Mark 2E, Mark 2F, Mark 3, Mark 3A, Mark 3B or Mark 4 coaches. Class 55 locomotives provide an e.t.s. directly from one of their traction generators into the train line. Consequently voltage fluctuations can result in motor-alternator flashover. Thus these locomotives are not suitable for use with Mark 2D, Mark 2E, Mark 2F, Mark 3, Mark 3A, Mark 3B or Mark 4 coaches unless modified motor-alternators are fitted. Such motor alternators were fitted to Mark 2D and 2F coaches used on the East Coast main line, but few remain fitted.

BUILD DETAILS

Lot Numbers

Vehicles ordered under the auspices of BR were allocated a lot (batch) number when ordered and these are quoted in class headings and sub-headings.

Builders

These are shown in class headings, the following abbreviations being used:

ABB Derby	ABB, Derby Carriage Works (now Bombardier Derby).
ABB York	ABB, York.
Adtranz Derby	Adtranz, Derby (now Bombardier Derby)..
Alstom Birmingham	Alstom, Saltley, Birmingham.
Alstom Eastleigh	Alstom, Eastleigh Works.
Ashford	BR, Ashford Works.
BRCW	Birmingham Railway Carriage & Wagon Company., Smethwick, Birmingham.
BREL Derby	BREL, Derby Carriage Works (later ABB/Adtranz Derby, now Bombardier Derby).
Charles Roberts	Charles Roberts and Company., Horbury, Wakefield (now Bombardier Transportaion)
Cravens	Cravens, Sheffield.
Derby	BR, Derby Carriage Works (later BREL Derby, then ABB / Adtranz Derby, now Bombardier Derby).
Doncaster	BR, Doncaster Works (later BREL Doncaster, then BRML Doncaster, then ABB/Adtranz Doncaster, now Bombardier)
Eastleigh	BR, Eastleigh Works (later BREL Eastleigh, then Wessex Traincare, now Alstom Eastleigh).
Glasgow	BR Springburn Works, Glasgow (now Alstom, Glasgow)
Gloucester	The Gloucester Railway Carriage & Wagon Co.
Hunslet-Barclay	Hunslet Barclay, Kilmarnock Works
Metro-Cammell	Metropolitan-Cammell, Saltley, Birmingham (later GEC-Alsthom Birmingham, now Alstom Birmingham).

Pressed Steel	Pressed Steel, Linwood.
Railcare Wolverton	Railcare, Wolverton (now Alstom).
Swindon	BR Swindon Works
Wessex Traincare	Wessex Traincare, Eastleigh Works (later Alstom Eastleigh).
Wolverton	BR Wolverton Works (later BREL Wolverton then Railcare, Wolverton, now Alstom Wolverton).
York	BR, York Carriage Works (later BREL York, then ABB York).

Information on sub-contracting works which built parts of vehicles e.g.the underframes etc. is not shown.

In addition to the above, certain vintage Pullman cars were built or rebuilt at the following works:

Metropolitan Carriage & Wagon Company, Birmingham (Now Alstom)
Midland Carriage & Wagon Company, Birmingham
Pullman Car Company, Preston Park, Brighton

Conversions have also been carried out at the Railway Technical Centre, Derby, BR Salisbury Depot and Blakes Fabrications, Edinburgh.

Vehicle Numbers
Where a coach has been renumbered, the former number is shown in parentheses. If a coach has been renumbered more than once, the original number is shown first in parentheses, followed by the most recent previous number. Where the former number of a coach due to be converted or renumbered is known and the conversion and/or renumbering has not yet taken place, the coach is listed under both current number (with depot allocation) and under new number (without allocation).

Numbering Systems
Seven different numbering systems were in use on BR. These were the BR series, the four pre-nationalisation companies' series', the Pullman Car Company's series and the UIC (International Union of Railways) series. BR number series coaches and former Pullman Car Company series are listed separately. There is also a separate listing of 'Saloon' type vehicles which are registered to run on the Railtrack network. Please note the Mark 2 Pullman vehicles were ordered after the Pullman Car Company had been nationalised and are therefore numbered in the BR series.

THE DEVELOPMENT OF BR STANDARD COACHES

The standard BR coach built from 1951 to 1963 was the Mark 1. This type features a separate underframe and body. The underframe is normally 64 ft. 6 in. long, but certain vehicles were built on shorter (57 ft.) frames. Tungsten lighting was standard and until 1961, BR Mark 1 bogies were generally provided. In 1959 Lot No. 30525 (TSO) appeared with fluorescent lighting and melamine interior panels, and from 1961 onwards Commonwealth bogies were fitted in an attempt to improve the quality of ride which became very poor when the tyre profiles on the wheels of the BR1 bogies became worn. Later batches of TSO and BSO retained the features of Lot No. 30525, but compartment vehicles – whilst utilising melamine panelling in standard class – still retained tungsten lighting. Wooden interior finish was retained in first class vehicles where the only change was to fluorescent lighting in open vehicles (except Lot No. 30648, which had tungsten lighting). In later years many Mark 1 coaches had BR 1 bogies replaced by B4.

In 1964, a new prototype train was introduced. Known as 'XP64', it featured new seat designs, pressure heating & ventilation, aluminium compartment doors and corridor partitions, foot pedal operated toilets and B4 bogies. The vehicles were built on standard Mark 1 underframes. Folding exterior doors were fitted, but these proved troublesome and were later replaced with hinged doors. All XP64 coaches have been withdrawn, but some have been preserved.

The prototype Mark 2 vehicle (W 13252) was produced in 1963. This was an FK of semi-integral construction and had pressure heating & ventilation, tungsten lighting, and was mounted on B4 bogies. This vehicle has been preserved by the National Railway Museum and is currently on display at Swindon. The production build was similar, but wider windows were used. The TSO and SO vehicles used a new seat design similar to that in the XP64 and fluorescent lighting was provided. Interior finish reverted to wood. Mark 2 vehicles were built from 1964–66.

The Mark 2A design, built 1967–68, incorporated the remainder of the features first used in the XP64 coaches, i.e. foot pedal operated toilets (except BSO), new first class seat design, aluminium compartment doors and partitions together with fluorescent lighting in first class compartments. Folding gangway doors (lime green coloured) were used instead of the traditional one-piece variety.

The following list summarises the changes made in the later Mark 2 variants:

Mark 2B: Wide wrap around doors at vehicle ends, no centre doors, slightly longer body. In standard class, one toilet at each end instead of two at one end as previously. Red folding gangway doors.

Mark 2C: Lowered ceiling with twin strips of fluorescent lighting and ducting for air conditioning, but air conditioning not fitted.

Mark 2D: Air conditioning. No opening top-lights in windows.

Mark 2E: Smaller toilets with luggage racks opposite. Fawn folding gangway doors.

Mark 2F: Plastic interior panels. Inter-City 70 type seats. Modified air conditioning system.

The Mark 3 design has BT10 bogies, is 75 ft. (23 m.) long and is of fully integral construction with Inter-City 70 type seats. Gangway doors were yellow (red in RFB) when new, although these are being changed on refurbishment. Loco-hauled coaches are classified Mark 3A, Mark 3 being reserved for HST trailers. A new batch of FO and BFO, classified Mark 3B, was built in 1985 with Advanced Passenger Train-style seating and revised lighting. The last vehicles in the Mark 3 series were the driving brake vans built for West Coast Main Line services.

The Mark 4 design was built by Metro-Cammell for use on the East Coast Main Line after electrification and features a body profile suitable for tilting trains, although tilt is not fitted, and is not intended to be. This design is suitable for 140 m.p.h. running, although is restricted to 125 m.p.h. because the signalling system on the route is not suitable for the higher speed. The bogies for these coaches were built by SIG in Switzerland and are designated BT41. Power operated sliding plug exterior doors are standard.

1. BR NUMBER SERIES STOCK PASSENGER STOCK

AJ11 (RF) RESTAURANT FIRST

Dia. AJ106. Mark 1. 325 spent most of its life as a Royal Train vehicle and was numbered 2907 for a time. Built with Commonwealth bogies, but B5 bogies substituted on 325. 24/–. ETH 2.

Lot No. 30633 Swindon 1961. 42.5 t C, 41 t B5.

324	x	**CH**	NY	*SS*	NY
325		**PC**	VS	*SS*	SL

AP1Z (PFK) PULLMAN FIRST WITH KITCHEN

Dia. AP101. Mark 2. Pressure Ventilated. 18/– 2T. B5 bogies. ETH 6.

Lot No. 30755 Derby 1966. 40 t.

504	**PC**	WC	*SS*	CS	ULLSWATER
506	**PC**	WC	*SS*	CS	WINDERMERE

AQ1Z (PFP) PULLMAN PARLOUR FIRST

Dia. AQ101. Mark 2. Pressure Ventilated. 36/– 2T. B4 bogies. ETH 5.

Lot No. 30754 Derby 1966. 35 t.

546	**PC**	WC	*SS*	CS	CONISTON WATER
548	**PC**	WC	*SS*	CS	GRASMERE
549	**PC**	WC	*SS*	CS	BASSENTHWAITE LAKE
550	**PC**	WC	*SS*	CS	RYDAL WATER
551	**PC**	WC	*SS*	CS	BUTTERMERE
552	**PC**	WC	*SS*	CS	ENNERDALE WATER
553	**PC**	WC	*SS*	CS	CRUMMOCK WATER

AR1Z (PFB) PULLMAN BRAKE FIRST

Dia. AR101. Mark 2. Pressure Ventilated. 30/– 2T. B4 bogies. ETH 4.

Lot No. 30753 Derby 1966. 35 t.

586	**PC**	WC	*SS*	CS	DERWENTWATER

AJ21 (RG) GRIDDLE CAR

Dia. AJ210. Mark 1. Rebuilt from RF. –/30. B5 bogies. ETH 2.

This vehicle was numbered DB975878 for a time when in departmental service for British Railways.

Lot No. 30013 Doncaster 1952. Rebuilt Wolverton 1965. 40 t.

1105	(302)	v	**G**	MH	*SS*	RL

AJ1F (RFB) BUFFET OPEN FIRST

Dia. AJ104. Mark 2F. Air conditioned. Converted 1988–9/91 at BREL, Derby from Mark 2F FOs. 1200/1/3/6/11/14–17/20/21/50/2/5/6/9 have Stones equipment, others have Temperature Ltd. 25/– 1T 1W (except 1217 and 1253 which are 26/ – 1T). B4 bogies. p. q. d. ETH 6X.

1200/3/6/11/14/16/20/52/5/6. Lot No. 30845 Derby 1973. 33 t.
1201/4/5/7/8/10/12/13/15/17–9/21/50/1/4/7/9. Lot No. 30859 Derby 1973–74. 33 t.
1202/9/53/8. Lot No. 30873 Derby 1974–75. 33 t.

† Fitted with new m.a. sets.

1200	(3287, 6459)	†	**V**	H	*VX*	MA
1201	(3361, 6445)	†	**V**	H	*VX*	MA
1202	(3436, 6456)	†	**V**	H	*VX*	MA
1203	(3291)	†		H	*VX*	MA
1204	(3401)	†	**V**	H	*VX*	MA
1205	(3329, 6438)	†	**V**	H	*VX*	MA
1206	(3319)	†	**V**	H	*VX*	MA
1207	(3328, 6422)	†	**V**	H	*VX*	MA
1208	(3393)		**V**	H	*VX*	MA
1209	(3437, 6457)	†	**V**	H	*VX*	MA
1210	(3405, 6462)	†	**V**	H	*VX*	MA
1211	(3305)			H	*VX*	MA
1212	(3427, 6453)	†	**V**	H	*VX*	MA
1213	(3419)	†	**V**	H	*VX*	MA
1214	(3317, 6433)			H	*VX*	MA
1215	(3377)			H	*VX*	MA
1216	(3302)	†	**V**	H	*VX*	MA
1217	(3357, 6444)		**CS**	H	*SR*	IS
1218	(3332)		**AR**	H	*AR*	NC
1219	(3418)		**AR**	H	*AR*	NC
1220	(3315, 6432)	†	**V**	H	*VX*	MA
1221	(3371)			H	*VX*	MA
1250	(3372)	†	**V**	H	*VX*	MA
1251	(3383)	†	**V**	H	*VX*	MA
1252	(3280)	†	**V**	H	*VX*	MA
1253	(3432)	†	**V**	H	*VX*	MA
1254	(3391)	†	**V**	H	*VX*	MA
1255	(3284)	†	**V**	H	*VX*	MA
1256	(3296)	†		H	*VX*	MA
1258	(3322)	†	**V**	H	*VX*	MA
1259	(3439)	†	**V**	H	*VX*	MA
1260	(3378)	†	**V**	H	*VX*	MA

AK51 (RKB) KITCHEN BUFFET

Dia. AK502. Mark 1. No seats. B5 bogies. ETH 1.

Lot No. 30624 Cravens 1960–61. 41 t.

1566	**M**	VS	*SS*	CP

AJ41 (RBR) RESTAURANT BUFFET

Dia. AJ403. Mark 1. Built with 23 loose chairs (Dia. AJ402). All remaining vehicles refurbished with 23 fixed polypropylene chairs and fluorescent lighting. ETH 2 (2X*).

r Further refurbished with 21 chairs, payphone, wheelchair space and carpets (Dia. AJ416).
s Modified for use as servery vehicle with 14 chairs (1680) or 8 chairs (1698).

1651–1699. Lot No. 30628 Pressed Steel 1960–61. Commonwealth bogies. 39 t.
1730. Lot No. 30512 BRCW 1960–61. B5 bogies. 37 t.

Non-standard Livery: 1680 and 1698 are British racing green & cream.

1651		**BR**	RV		CP
1653			RS		FP
1658		**BG**	RS	*SS*	BN
1659	x	**PC**	WT	*SS*	RL
1671	x*	**CC**	RS	*SS*	BN
1674			RS	*SS*	BN
1679		**G**	RS	*SS*	BN
1680	x*s	**0**	RS	*SS*	BN
1683	r	**BR**	RV	*SS*	CP
1691	r	**G**	H		CP
1692	xr	**CH**	RV	*SS*	CP
1696		**G**	RS	*SS*	BN
1697	r		H		CP
1698	s	**0**	RS	*SS*	BN
1699	r		H		CP
1730	x	**M**	BK	*SS*	BT

AN21 (RMB) MINIATURE BUFFET CAR

Dia. AN203. Mark 1. –/44 2T. These vehicles are basically an open standard with two full window spaces removed to accommodate a buffet counter, and four seats removed to allow for a stock cupboard. All remaining vehicles now have fluorescent lighting. All vehicles have Commonwealth bogies except 1850 (B5). ETH 3.

1813–1832. Lot No. 30520 Wolverton 1960. 38 t.
1840–1850. Lot No. 30507 Wolverton 1960. 37 t (1850 is 36 t).
1859–1863. Lot No. 30670 Wolverton 1961–62. 38 t.
1871–1882. Lot No. 30702 Wolverton 1962. 38 t.

1842/50/71 have been refurbished and are fitted with a microwave oven and payphone. Dia. AN208.

1813	x	**CC**	RS	*SS*	BN
1832	x	**BG**	RS	*SS*	BN
1840	v	**G**	MH	*SS*	RL
1842	x	**CH**	H		CP
1850			H		CP
1859	x	**M**	BK	*SS*	BT
1860	x	**M**	WC	*SS*	CS
1861	x	**CH**	WC	*SS*	TM
1863	x	**CH**	RV	*SS*	CP
1871	x		H		BQ
1882	x	**M**	WC	*SS*	CS

AJ41 (RBR) RESTAURANT BUFFET

Dia. AJ414. Mark 1. These vehicles were built as unclassified restaurant (RU). They were rebuilt with buffet counters and 23 fixed polypropylene chairs (RBS), then further refurbished by fitting fluorescent lighting and reclassified RBR. ETH 2X.

1953. Lot No. 30575 Swindon 1960. B4/B5 bogies. 36.5 t.
1981. Lot No. 30632 Swindon 1961. Commonwealth bogies. 39 t.

1953 **M** VS *SS* CP
1981 **M** FR *SS* TM

AS41 FIRST CLASS SLEEPING CAR

Dia. AS101. Mark 1. Pressure Ventilated. 11 single-berth compartments plus an attendant's compartment. ETH 3 (3X*).

2013. Lot No. 30159 Wolverton 1958. B5 bogies. 39 t.
2127. Lot No. 30687 Wolverton 1961. Commonwealth bogies. 41 t.

2013 was numbered 2908 for a time when in use with the Royal Train.

2013 **M** FS SZ | 2127 * **M** GS CS

AU51 CHARTER TRAIN STAFF COACHES

Dia. AU501. Mark 1. Converted from BCKs in 1988. Commonwealth bogies. ETH 2.

Lot No. 30732 Derby 1964. 37 t.

Non-standard Livery: 2834 is British racing green & cream.

2833 (21270) **BG** RS *SS* BN | 2834 (21267) **0** RS *SS* BN

AT5G HM THE QUEEN'S SALOON

Dia. AT525. Mark 3. Converted from a FO built 1972. Consists of a lounge, bedroom and bathroom for HM The Queen, and a combined bedroom and bathroom for the Queen's dresser. One entrance vestibule has double doors. Air conditioned. BT10 bogies. ETH 9X.

Lot No. 30886 Wolverton 1977. 36 t.

2903 (11001) **RP** RK *RP* ZN

AT5G HRH THE DUKE OF EDINBURGH'S SALOON

Dia. AT526. Mark 3. Converted from a TSO built 1972. Consists of a combined lounge/dining room, a bedroom and a shower room for the Duke, a kitchen and a valet's bedroom and bathroom. Air conditioned. BT10 bogies. ETH 15X.

Lot No. 30887 Wolverton 1977. 36 t.

2904 (12001) **RP** RK *RP* ZN

AT5B ROYAL HOUSEHOLD COUCHETTE

Dia. AT528. Mark 2B. Converted from a BFK built 1969. Consists of luggage accommodation, guards compartment and staff accommodation. Pressure ventilated. B5 bogies. ETH 4X.

Lot No. 30889 Wolverton 1977. 35.5 t.

2906 (14112) **RP** RK DY

AT5G ROYAL HOUSEHOLD SLEEPING CAR

Dia. AT531. Mark 3A. Built to similar specification as SLE 10646–732. 12 sleeping compartments for use of Royal Household with a fixed lower berth and a hinged upper berth. 2T plus shower room. Air conditioned. BT10 bogies. ETH 11X.

Lot No. 31002 Derby/Wolverton 1985. 44 t.

2915 **RP** RK *RP* ZN

AT5G ROYAL KITCHEN/DINING CAR

Dia. AT537. Mark 3. Converted from HST TRUK built 1976. Large kitchen retained, but dining area modified for Royal use seating up to 14 at central table(s). Air conditioned. BT10 bogies. ETH 13X.

Lot No. 31059 Wolverton 1988. 43 t.

2916 (40512) **RP** RK *RP* ZN

AT5G ROYAL HOUSEHOLD KITCHEN/DINING CAR

Dia. AT539. Mark 3. Converted from HST TRUK built 1977. Large kitchen retained and dining area slightly modified with seating for 22 Royal Household members. Air conditioned. BT10 bogies. ETH 13X.

Lot No. 31084 Wolverton 1990. 43 t.

2917 (40514) **RP** RK *RP* ZN

AT5G ROYAL HOUSEHOLD CARS

Dia. AT538 (AT540*). Mark 3. Converted from HST TRUKs built 1976/7. Air conditioned. BT10 bogies. ETH 10X.

Lot Nos. 31083 (31085*) Wolverton 1989. 41.05 t.

2918 (40515) **RP** RK ZN
2919 (40518) * **RP** RK ZN

AT5B ROYAL HOUSEHOLD COUCHETTES

Dia. AT536. Mark 2B. Converted from BFK built 1969. Consists of luggage accommodation, guard's compartment, workshop area, 350 kW diesel generator and staff sleeping accommodation. B5 bogies. ETH2X.

Lot No. 31044 Wolverton 1986. 48 t.

2920 (14109, 17109) **RP** RK *RP* ZN

Dia. AT541. Mark 2B. Converted from BFK built 1969. Consists of luggage accommodation, kitchen, brake control equipment and staff accommodation. B5 bogies. ETH7X.

Lot No. 31086 Wolverton 1990. 41.5 t.

2921 (14107, 17107) **RP** RK *RP* ZN

AT5G HRH THE PRINCE OF WALES'S SLEEPING CAR

Dia. AT534. Mark 3B. BT10 bogies. Air conditioned.ETH 7X.

Lot No. 31035 Derby/Wolverton 1987.

2922 **RP** RK *RP* ZN

AT5G HRH THE PRINCE OF WALES'S SALOON

Dia. AT535. Mark 3B. BT10 bogies. Air conditioned. ETH 6X.

Lot No. 31036 Derby/Wolverton 1987.

2923 **RP** RK *RP* ZN

AD11 (FO) OPEN FIRST

Dia. AD103. Mark 1. 42/– 2T. ETH 3. Many now fitted with table lamps.

3063–3069. Lot No. 30169 Doncaster 1955. B4 bogies. 33 t.
3096–3100. Lot No. 30576 BRCW 1959. B4 bogies. 33 t.

3064 and 3068 were numbered DB 975607 and DB 975606 for a time when in departmental service for British Rail.

3063	**BG**	VS		SL
3064	**BG**	VS		SL
3066	**RB**	VS	*SS*	CP
3068	**RB**	VS	*SS*	CP
3069	**RB**	VS	*SS*	CP
3096	x **M**	BK	*SS*	BT
3097	**0**	RS	*SS*	BN
3098	x **CH**	RV	*SS*	CP
3100	x **CC**	RS	*SS*	BN

Later design with fluorescent lighting, aluminium window frames and Commonwealth bogies.

3105–3128. Lot No. 30697 Swindon 1962–63. 36 t.
3130–3150. Lot No. 30717 Swindon 1963. 36 t.

3128/36/41/3/4/6/7/8 were renumbered 1058/60/3/5/6/8/9/70 when reclassified RUO, then 3600/5/8/9/2/6/4/10 when declassified, but have since regained their original numbers.

Mark 1 Stock. Restaurant buffet (RBR) 1696, now in use as a kitchen car in SR green livery with Commonwealth bogies at Worcester Shrub Hill on 02/12/2000.
Stephen Widdowson

▲ Open first (FO) 3125 'LOCH SHIEL' at Ayr 14/07/2001. **Stephen Widdowson**

▼ Open standard (TSO) 4963 in chocolate and cream livery at Gloucester on 28/09/2001. **Stephen Widdowson**

AX51 Generator Van 6311 on B4 bogies in plain blue livery at Worcester Shrub Hill on 02/12/2000. **Stephen Widdowson**

▲ **Mark 2A Stock.** Open standard (TSO) 5376 'MICHAELA' at Wooferton on 12/05/2001. This coach is in HSBC livery. **Bob Sweet**

▼ Corridor brake first (BFK) No. 17056 at Kidderminster on 08/07/2001. **Stephen Widdowson**

Mark 2D Stock. Open first with miniature buffet (RMBF) 6723 **(above)** and Brake open standard (BSO) 9492 **(below)** in Great Western livery at Plymouth on 28/05/2001. **Stephen Widdowson (2)**

▲ **Mark 2E Stock.** Open first (FO) 3252 at Reading on 22/06/2001 in the formation of the 08.20 Penzance–London Paddington. **Kevin Conkey**

▼ Open standard (TSO) 5887, still in InterCity livery seen passing Dawlish on 25/08/2001. **Stephen Widdowson**

Mark 2F Stock. Buffet first (RFB) 1214, still in InterCity livery in a Virgin Cross-Country train on 06/07/2000. **Mark Beal**

▲ Open standard (TSO) 6106 in Virgin livery at Stafford on 24/06/2001.
Hugh Ballantyne

▼ Driving brake open standard (DBSO) 9701 at Ipswich on 08/06/2001.
Mark Beal

Non-standard Livery: 3097, 3120/21/41/46/47/49 are British racing green & cream.

3105	x	**M**	WC	*SS*	CS
3107	x	**BG**	RS	*SS*	BN
3110	x	**CC**	RS	*SS*	BN
3112	x	**CH**	RV	*SS*	CP
3113	x	**M**	WC	*SS*	CS
3114		**G**	RS	*SS*	BN
3115	x	**BG**	RS	*SS*	BN
3117	x	**M**	WC	*SS*	CS
3119	x	**CC**	RS	*SS*	BN
3120		**0**	RS	*SS*	BN
3121		**0**	RS	*SS*	BN
3122	x	**CH**	RV	*SS*	CP
3123		**G**	RS	*SS*	BN
3124		**G**	RS	*SS*	BN
3125		**RB**	VS	*SS*	CP
3127		**G**	RS	*SS*	BN
3128	x	**M**	WC	*SS*	CS
3130	v	**M**	WC	*SS*	CS
3131	x	**CC**	RS	*SS*	BN
3132	x	**CC**	RS	*SS*	BN
3133	x	**CC**	RS	*SS*	BN
3136			SO	*SO*	ZA
3140	x	**CH**	RV	*SS*	CP
3141		**0**	RS	*SS*	BN
3143			WC	*SS*	CS
3144	x	**CC**	RS	*SS*	BN
3146		**0**	RS	*SS*	BN
3147		**0**	RS	*SS*	BN
3148		**BG**	RS	*SS*	BN
3149		**0**	RS	*SS*	BN
3150		**G**	RS	*SS*	BN

AD1D (FO) OPEN FIRST

Dia. AD105. Mark 2D. Air conditioned. 3172–88 have Stones equipment. 3192/3202 have Temperature Ltd. 42/– 2T. B4 bogies. ETH 5.

Lot No. 30821 Derby 1971–72. 32.5 t.

3172		RK	*SO*	DY
3174	**VN**	VS	*SS*	CP
3178		VS		CP
3181	**RB**	RV	*SS*	CP
3182	**VN**	VS	*SS*	CP
3186		RS		DY
3187		E		CL
3188	**RB**	RV	*SS*	CP
3192		RK	*SO*	DY
3202		E		CL

AD1E (FO) OPEN FIRST

Dia. AD106. Mark 2E. Air conditioned. Stones equipment. 42/– 2T (41/– 2T 1W w). B4 bogies. ETH 5.

* Seats removed to accommodate catering module. 40F 1T.
r Refurbished with new seats.
u Fitted with power supply for Mk. 1 RBR.

3255 was numbered 3525 for a time when fitted with a pantry.

Lot No. 30843 Derby 1972–73. 32.5 t.

Non-standard Livery: 3231 & 3246 are British racing green & cream.

3223		**RB**	RV	*SS*	CP
3225			E		KT
3226			E		KT
3228	du	**RB**	H		CP
3229	d		H		CP
3230			RK	*SO*	DY
3231		**0**	RA		CP
3232	dr	**FG**	H	*GW*	OO

3234	w		VS		CP
3235	u		H		PY
3237			RS		FP
3239			VS		CP
3240		**RB**	RV	*SS*	CP
3241	dr	**FG**	H	*GW*	OO
3242	wu		H		PY
3244	d	**RB**	H		CP
3246	w	**0**	RA		CP
3247		**VN**	VS	*SS*	CP
3248			RK	*SO*	DY
3251	*		RS		FP
3252	w		H		PY
3255	dr	**FG**	H	*GW*	OO
3256	w		H		PY
3257	w		VS		CP
3258	n		E		KT
3261	dw	**FG**	H	*GW*	OO
3267		**VN**	VS	*SS*	CP
3268			RV		CP
3269	dr	**FG**	H	*GW*	OO
3270			VS		CP
3272			VS		CP
3273		**VN**	VS	*SS*	CP
3275		**VN**	VS	*SS*	CP

AD1F (FO) OPEN FIRST

Dia. AD107. Mark 2F. Air conditioned. 3277–3318/58–81 have Stones equipment, others have Temperature Ltd. 42/– 2T. All now refurbished with power-operated vestibule doors, new panels and new seat trim. B4 bogies. d. ETH 5X.

3277–3318. Lot No. 30845 Derby 1973. 33 t.
3325–3428. Lot No. 30859 Derby 1973–74. 33 t.
3429–3438. Lot No. 30873 Derby 1974–75. 33 t.

r Further refurbished with table lamps, modified seats with burgundy seat trim and new m.a. sets.
s Further refurbished with table lamps and modified seats with burgundy seat trim.
u Fitted with power supply for Mk. 1 RBR.

3403 was numbered 6450 for a time when declassified.

3277		**AR**	H	*AR*	NC
3278	r	**V**	H	*VW*	OY
3279	u	**AR**	H	*AR*	NC
3285	s	**V**	H	*VW*	OY
3290		**AR**	H	*AR*	NC
3292			H	*AR*	NC
3293			H	*VL*	CF
3295		**AR**	H	*AR*	NC
3299	r	**V**	H	*VW*	OY
3300	s	**V**	H	*VW*	OY
3303		**AR**	H	*AR*	NC
3304	r	**V**	H	*VW*	OY
3309			H	*AR*	NC
3312			H	*AR*	NC
3313	r	**V**	H	*VW*	OY
3314	r	**V**	H	*VW*	OY
3318			H	*AR*	NC
3325	r	**V**	H	*VW*	OY
3326	r	**V**	H	*VW*	OY
3330	r	**V**	H	*VW*	OY
3331		**AR**	H	*AR*	NC
3333	r	**V**	H	*VW*	OY
3334		**AR**	H	*AR*	NC
3336	u	**AR**	H	*AR*	NC
3337	r	**V**	H	*VW*	OY
3338	u	**AR**	H	*AR*	NC
3340	r	**V**	H	*VW*	OY
3344	r	**V**	H	*VW*	OY
3345	r	**V**	H	*VW*	OY
3348	r	**V**	H	*VW*	OY
3350	r	**V**	H	*VW*	OY
3351		**AR**	H	*AR*	NC
3352	r	**V**	H	*VW*	OY
3353	s	**V**	H	*VW*	OY
3354	s	**V**	H	*VW*	OY
3356	r	**V**	H	*VW*	OY
3358		**AR**	H	*AR*	NC
3359	s	**V**	H	*VW*	OY
3360	s	**V**	H	*VW*	OY
3362	s	**V**	H	*VW*	OY

3363	s	**V**	H	*VW*	OY
3364	r	**V**	H	*VW*	OY
3366	s	**V**	H	*VW*	OY
3368		**AR**	H	*AR*	NC
3369	s	**V**	H	*VW*	OY
3373			H		MB
3374			H	*AR*	NC
3375		**AR**	H	*AR*	NC
3379	u	**AR**	H	*AR*	NC
3381			H		MB
3384	r	**V**	H	*VW*	OY
3385	r	**V**	H	*VW*	OY
3386	r	**V**	H	*VW*	OY
3387	s	**V**	H	*VW*	OY
3388		**AR**	H	*AR*	NC
3389	s	**V**	H	*VW*	OY
3390	r	**V**	H	*VW*	OY
3392	r	**V**	H	*VW*	OY
3395	r	**V**	H	*VW*	OY
3397	r	**V**	H	*VW*	OY
3399	u	**AR**	H	*AR*	NC
3400		**AR**	H	*AR*	NC
3402	s	**V**	H	*VW*	OY
3403	s	**V**	H	*VW*	OY
3408	s	**V**	H	*VW*	OY
3411	s	**V**	H	*VW*	OY
3414		**AR**	H	*AR*	NC
3416			H	*AR*	NC
3417		**AR**	H	*AR*	NC
3424		**AR**	H	*AR*	NC
3425	s	**V**	H	*VW*	OY
3426	r	**V**	H	*VW*	OY
3428	s	**V**	H	*VW*	OY
3429	r	**V**	H	*VW*	OY
3431	r	**V**	H	*VW*	OY
3433	r	**V**	H	*VW*	OY
3434	s	**V**	H	*VW*	OY
3438	s	**V**	H	*VW*	OY

AG1E (FO (T)) OPEN FIRST (PANTRY)

Dia. AG101. Mark 2E. Air conditioned. Converted from FO. Fitted with pantry containing microwave oven and space for a trolley. 36/– 2T. B4 bogies. p. d. ETH 5X.

Lot No. 30843 Derby 1972–73. 32.5 t.

3520	(3253)	**FG**	H	*GW*	OO
3521	(3271)	**AR**	H	*AR*	NC
3522	(3236)	**FG**	H	*GW*	OO
3523	(3238)		H		ZN
3524	(3254)		H		IS

AC21 (TSO) OPEN STANDARD

Dia. AC204. Mark 1. These vehicles have 2+2 seating and are classified TSO ('Tourist second open'– a former LNER designation). –/64 2T. ETH 4.

3766. Lot No. 30079 York 1953. Commonwealth bogies (originally built with BR Mark 1 bogies). This coach has narrower seats than later vehicles. 36 t.
4198. Lot No. 30172 York 1956. BR Mark 1 bogies. 33 t.

3766	x	**M**	WC	*SS*	CS
4198	v	**CH**	NY	*SS*	NY

AD21 (SO) OPEN STANDARD

Dia. AD201. Mark 1. These vehicles have 2+1 seating and were often used as second class dining cars when new. –/48 2T. BR Mark 1 bogies. ETH 4.

4786. Lot No. 30376 York 1957. 33 t.
4817. Lot No. 30473 BRCW 1957–59. 33 t.

4786	v	**CH**	NY	*SS*	NY
4817	v	**CH**	NY	*SS*	NY

AC21 (TSO) OPEN STANDARD

Dia. AC201. Mark 1. These vehicles are a development of Dia. AC204 with fluorescent lighting and modified design of seat headrest. Built with BR Mark 1 bogies. –/64 2T. ETH 4.

4832–4836. Lot No. 30506 Wolverton 1959. Commonwealth bogies. 33 t.
4849–4880. Lot No. 30525 Wolverton 1959–60. B4 bogies. 33 t.

4832	x	**M**	BK	*SS*	BT
4836	x	**M**	BK	*SS*	BT
4849		**RR**	H		KT
4854		**RR**	H		KT
4856	x	**M**	BK	*SS*	BT
4866		**RR**	H		KT
4873		**RR**	H		BQ
4875		**RR**	H		KT
4876		**RR**	H		KT
4880		**RR**	H		KT

Lot No. 30646 Wolverton 1961. Built with Commonwealth bogies, but BR Mark 1 bogies substituted by the SR on 4902/5/12/15/16. All now re-rebogied. 34 t B4, 36 t C.

4902	x B4	**CH**	RV	*SS*	CP
4905	x C	**M**	WC	*SS*	TM
4912	x C	**M**	WC	*SS*	CS
4915	x B4	**CC**	RS	*SS*	BN
4916	x B4	**CC**	RS	*SS*	BN
4917	x C	**RR**	H		BQ

Lot No. 30690 Wolverton 1961–62. Commonwealth bogies and aluminium window frames. 37 t.

4925		**G**	RS	*SS*	BN
4927	x	**CH**	RV	*SS*	CP
4931	v	**M**	WC	*SS*	CS
4938		**BG**	RS	*SS*	BN
4939			SO	*SO*	ZA
4940	x	**M**	WC	*SS*	CS
4946	x	**CC**	RS	*SS*	BN
4949		**BG**	RS	*SS*	BN
4951	x	**M**	WC	*SS*	CS
4954	v	**M**	WC	*SS*	CS
4956		**BG**	RS	*SS*	BN
4958	v	**M**	WC	*SS*	CS
4959		**BG**	RS	*SS*	BN
4960	x	**M**	WC	*SS*	TM
4963	x	**CH**	RV	*SS*	CP
4973	x	**M**	WC	*SS*	TM
4977		**G**	RS	*SS*	BN
4984	v	**M**	WC	*SS*	CS
4986		**G**	RS	*SS*	BN
4991		**BG**	RS	*SS*	BN
4994	x	**M**	WC	*SS*	CS
4996	x	**CC**	RS	*SS*	BN
4998		**BG**	RS	*SS*	BN
4999		**BG**	RS	*SS*	BN
5002		**BG**	RS	*SS*	BN
5005		**BG**	RS	*SS*	BN
5007		**G**	RS	*SS*	BN
5008	x	**CC**	RS	*SS*	BN
5009	x	**CH**	RV	*SS*	CP
5023		**G**	RS	*SS*	BN
5025	x	**CH**	RV	*SS*	CP
5027		**G**	RS	*SS*	BN
5028	x	**M**	BK	*SS*	BT
5029	x	**CH**	RV	*SS*	CP
5030	x	**CH**	RV	*SS*	CP
5032	x	**M**	WC	*SS*	CS
5033	x	**M**	WC	*SS*	CS
5035	x	**M**	WC	*SS*	CS
5037		**G**	RS	*SS*	BN
5040	x	**CH**	RV	*SS*	CP
5042	x		RS		FP
5044	x	**M**	WC	*SS*	CS

AC2Z (TSO) OPEN STANDARD

Dia. AC205. Mark 2. Pressure ventilated. –/64 2T. B4 bogies. ETH 4.

Lot No. 30751 Derby 1965–67. 32 t.

Note: 5157/77/91/98 are leased to Vintage Trains.

5125	v	**G**	MH	*SS*	RL
5132	v	**LN**	H		LT
5135	v	**RR**	H		LT
5148	v	**RR**	H		TM
5154	v	**LN**	H		LT
5156	v	**RR**	H		LT
5157	v	**CH**	H	*SS*	TM
5158	v	**RR**	H		LT
5161	v	**RR**	H		LT
5163	v	**RR**	H		LT
5167	v	**RR**	H		LT
5171	v	**G**	MH	*SS*	RL
5174	v	**RR**	H		LT
5177	v	**CH**	H	*SS*	TM
5179	v	**RR**	H		TM
5180	v	**RR**	H		LT
5183	v	**RR**	H		TM
5186	v	**RR**	H		TM
5191	v	**CH**	H	*SS*	TM
5193	v	**LN**	H		TM
5194	v	**RR**	H		TM
5198	v	**CH**	H	*SS*	TM
5200	v	**G**	MH	*SS*	RL
5207	v	**RR**	H		LT
5209	v	**RR**	H		LT
5212	v	**LN**	H		TM
5213	v	**RR**	H		LT
5216	v	**G**	MH	*SS*	RL
5221	v	**RR**	H		TM
5222	v	**G**	MH	*SS*	RL
5225	v	**RR**	H		LT
5226	v	**RR**	H		LT

AD2Z (SO) OPEN STANDARD

Dia. AD203. Mark 2. Pressure ventilated. –/48 2T. B4 bogies. ETH 4.

Lot No. 30752 Derby 1966. 32 t.

5236	v	**G**	MH	*SS*	RL
5237	v	**G**	MH	*SS*	RL
5249	v	**G**	MH	*SS*	RL

AC2A (TSO) OPEN STANDARD

Dia. AC206. Mark 2A. Pressure ventilated. –/64 2T (–/62 2T w). B4 bogies. ETH 4.

5265–5345. Lot No. 30776 Derby 1967–68. 32 t.
5350–5433. Lot No. 30787 Derby 1968. 32 t.

5265		**RR**	H		KT
5266		**RR**	RV		CP
5267		**RR**	H		KT
5271		**RR**	H		KT
5275		**RB**	RV	*SS*	CP
5276		**RB**	RV	*SS*	CP
5278		**RR**	H		KT
5282		**RR**	H		KT
5290		**NB**	H		KT
5292		**RB**	RV	*SS*	CP
5293		**NB**	H		KT
5299		**M**	WC	*SS*	CS
5304		**RR**	RV		CP
5307		**RB**	RV	*SS*	CP
5309		**RR**	H		CP
5322		**RR**	H		CP
5331		**RR**	H		CP
5335		**RR**	H		CP
5341		**RB**	RV	*SS*	CP
5345		**RR**	H		CP
5350		**RB**	RV	*SS*	CP
5353		**RR**	H		KT
5354		**RR**	H		PY
5364		**RB**	RV	*SS*	CP
5365		**RB**	RV	*SS*	CP
5366		**RB**	RV	*SS*	CP
5373		**RB**	RV	*SS*	CP
5376		**RB**	RV	*SS*	CP
5378		**RB**	RV	*SS*	CP
5379		**RR**	H		KT
5381	w	**RR**	H		CP
5384		**N**	RV		CP
5386	w	**RR**	H		CP
5389	w	**RR**	H		CP
5410		**N**	H		KT
5412	w	**RR**	H		KT

5419	w	**RR**	H		CP
5420	w	**RR**	H		CP
5433	w	**RR**	H		CP

AC2B (TSO) OPEN STANDARD

Dia. AC207. Mark 2B. Pressure ventilated. –/62 2T. B4 bogies. ETH 4.

Lot No. 30791 Derby 1969. 32 t.

5443		**N**	H		KT
5446		**N**	H		KT
5447		**N**	RV		CQ
5449		**N**	RV		CP
5450		**N**	RV		CP
5453	d	**M**	WC	*VL*	CF
5454		**N**	H		KT
5462		**N**	RV		CP
5463	d	**M**	WC	*VL*	CF
5464		**N**	RV		CP
5471		**N**	H		KT
5472		**N**	H		KT
5475		**N**	H		KT
5478	d	**M**	WC	*VL*	CF
5480		**N**	H		KT
5487	d	**M**	WC	*VL*	CF
5491	d	**M**	WC	*VL*	CF
5494		**N**	RV		CP

AC2C (TSO) OPEN STANDARD

Dia. AC208. Mark 2C. Pressure ventilated. –/62 2T. B4 bogies. ETH 4.

Lot No. 30795 Derby 1969–70. 32 t.

5554		**RR**	H		CP
5569	d	**M**	WC	*VL*	CF
5600		**M**	WC	*SS*	CS
5614		**RR**	H		CP

AC2D (TSO) OPEN STANDARD

Dia. AC209. Mark 2D. Air conditioned. Stones equipment. –/62 2T. B4 bogies. ETH 5.

Non-Standard Livery: 5630, 5732 & 5739 are **WV** without lining.

r Refurbished with new seats and end luggage stacks. –/58 2T.

Lot No. 30822 Derby 1971. 33 t.

5616			RS		FP
5618			H		PY
5620			H		PY
5623			H		PY
5629			H		PY
5630		**0**	RV	*SS*	CP
5631	dr	**FG**	H	*GW*	OO
5632	dr	**FG**	H	*GW*	OO
5636	dr	**FG**	H	*GW*	OO
5640			H		PY
5647		**RB**	RV	*SS*	CP
5650			H		PY
5657	dr	**FG**	H	*GW*	OO
5661			H		KT
5662			H		ZN
5663			H		KT
5669	dr	**FG**	H	*GW*	OO
5674			H		KT
5679	dr	**FG**	H	*GW*	OO
5687			H		KT
5690			H		PY
5694			H		KT
5699			H		KT
5700	dr	**FG**	H	*GW*	OO
5701			H		KT
5704		**M**	WC	*SS*	CS
5710	dr	**FG**	H	*GW*	OO
5711			H		PY
5714		**M**	WC	*SS*	CS
5715			H		PY
5716			H		KT
5718			H		KT

5722			E		CL
5724			H		PY
5726			H		PY
5727		**M**	WC	*SS*	CS
5728			H		PY
5731			H		KT
5732		**0**	RV	*SS*	CP
5737	dr	**FG**	H	*GW*	OO
5738			H		KT
5739		**0**	RV		CP
5740	dr	**FG**	H	*GW*	OO

AC2E (TSO) OPEN STANDARD

Dia. AC210. Mark 2E. Air conditioned. Stones equipment. –/64 2T (w –/62 2T 1W). B4 bogies. d (except 5756 and 5879). ETH 5.

5744–5801. Lot No. 30837 Derby 1972. 33.5 t.
5810–5906. Lot No. 30844 Derby 1972–73. 33.5 t.

r Refurbished with new interior panelling.
s Refurbished with new interior panelling, modified design of seat headrest and centre luggage stack. –/60 2T (w –/58 2T 1W).
t Refurbished with new interior panelling and new seats.

5744		**FG**	H	*GW*	OO
5745	s	**V**	H	*VX*	MA
5746	r	**V**	H	*VX*	MA
5748	r pt		H	*VX*	MA
5750	s	**V**	H	*VX*	MA
5752	wrpt		H	*VX*	MA
5754	ws	**V**	H	*VX*	MA
5756		**M**	WC	*SS*	CS
5769	r		H	*VX*	MA
5773	s pt	**V**	H	*VX*	MA
5775	s	**V**	H	*VX*	MA
5776	r		H	*VX*	MA
5778		**AR**	H	*AR*	NC
5779	r		H	*VX*	MA
5780		**AR**	H	*AR*	NC
5781		**AR**	H	*AR*	NC
5784	r	**V**	H	*VX*	MA
5787	s	**V**	H	*VX*	MA
5788	r		H	*VX*	MA
5789	r pt		H	*VX*	MA
5791	wr		H	*VX*	MA
5792	r		H	*VX*	MA
5793	wspt	**V**	H	*VX*	MA
5794	wr		H	*VX*	MA
5796	wr		H	*VX*	MA
5797	r		H	*VX*	MA
5800		**AR**	H	*AR*	NC
5801	r	**V**	H	*VX*	MA
5810	s	**V**	H	*VX*	MA
5812	wr		H	*VX*	MA
5814	r		H	*VX*	MA
5815	ws	**V**	H	*VX*	MA
5816	r pt		H	*VX*	MA
5821	r pt	**V**	H	*VX*	MA
5822	wspt	**V**	H	*VX*	MA
5824	rw		H	*VX*	MA
5827	r		H	*VX*	MA
5828	ws	**V**	H	*VX*	MA
5831		**AR**	H	*AR*	NC
5836		**AR**	H	*AR*	NC
5843	rw		H	*VX*	MA
5845	s	**V**	H	*VX*	MA
5847	rw	**V**	H	*VX*	MA
5852		**AR**	H	*AR*	NC
5853	t	**M**	H	*VL*	CF
5854	r		H	*VX*	MA
5859	s	**V**	H	*VX*	MA
5863		**AR**	H	*AR*	NC
5866	r pt		H	*VX*	MA
5868	s pt	**V**	H	*VX*	MA
5869	t	**M**	H	*VL*	CF
5874	t	**M**	H	*VL*	CF
5876	s pt	**V**	H	*VX*	MA
5879			RV		CP
5881	ws	**V**	H	*VX*	MA
5886	s	**V**	H	*VX*	MA
5887	wr		H	*VX*	MA
5888	wr		H	*VX*	MA
5889	s	**V**	H	*VX*	MA
5893	s	**V**	H	*VX*	MA
5897	r		H	*VX*	MA
5899	s	**V**	H	*VX*	MA
5900	wspt	**V**	H	*VX*	MA
5901	s	**V**	H	*VX*	MA

5902	s	**V**	H	*VX*	MA	5905	s	**V**	H	*VX*	MA
5903	s	**V**	H	*VX*	MA	5906	wspt		H	*VX*	MA

AC2F (TSO) OPEN STANDARD

Dia. AC211. Mark 2F. Air conditioned. Temperature Ltd. equipment. Inter-City 70 seats. All were refurbished in the 1980s with power-operated vestibule doors, new panels and new seat trim. –/64 2T. (w –/62 2T 1W) B4 bogies. d. ETH 5X.

5908–5958. Lot No. 30846 Derby 1973. 33 t.
5959–6170. Lot No. 30860 Derby 1973–74. 33 t.
6171–6184. Lot No. 30874 Derby 1974–75. 33 t.

* Early Mark 2 style seats.

These vehicles have undergone a second refurbishment with carpets and new seat trim .

Cross-Country vehicles:

r Standard refurbished vehicles with new m.a. sets.
s Also fitted with centre luggage stack. –/60 2T.
t Also fitted with centre luggage stack and wheelchair space. –/58 2T 1W.

West Coast vehicles:

r Standard refurbished vehicles with new seat trim and new m.a. sets.
u As 'r' but with two wheelchair spaces. –/60 2T 2W.
† Standard refurbished vehicles with new seat trim.

5908	r	**V**	H	*VW*	OY
5910	u	**V**	H	*VW*	OY
5911	s	**V**	H	*VX*	MA
5912	s	**V**	H	*VX*	MA
5913	s		H	*VX*	MA
5914	u	**V**	H	*VW*	OY
5915	r	**V**	H	*VW*	OY
5916	t		H	*VX*	MA
5917	s	**V**	H	*VX*	MA
5918	t	**V**	H	*VX*	MA
5919	s pt	**V**	H	*VX*	MA
5920	†	**V**	H	*VW*	OY
5921		**AR**	H	*AR*	NC
5922		**AR**	H	*AR*	NC
5924		**AR**	H	*AR*	NC
5925	s pt		H	*VX*	MA
5926			H	*AR*	NC
5927		**AR**	H	*AR*	NC
5928		**AR**	H	*AR*	NC
5929		**AR**	H	*AR*	NC
5930	t	**V**	H	*VX*	MA
5931	†w	**V**	H	*VW*	OY
5932	r	**V**	H	*VW*	OY
5933	r	**V**	H	*VW*	OY
5934	r	**V**	H	*VW*	OY
5935		**AR**	H	*AR*	NC
5936		**AR**	H	*AR*	NC
5937	r	**V**	H	*VW*	OY
5939	r	**V**	H	*VW*	OY
5940	u	**V**	H	*VW*	OY
5941	r	**V**	H	*VW*	OY
5943	rw	**V**	H	*VW*	OY
5944		**AR**	H	*AR*	NC
5945	r	**V**	H	*VW*	OY
5946	r	**V**	H	*VW*	OY
5947	s pt	**V**	H	*VX*	MA
5948	u	**V**	H	*VW*	OY
5949	u	**V**	H	*VW*	OY
5950		**AR**	H	*AR*	NC
5951	r	**V**	H	*VX*	MA
5952	r	**V**	H	*VW*	OY
5953	†	**V**	H	*VW*	OY
5954		**AR**	H	*AR*	NC
5955	r	**V**	H	*VW*	OY
5956			H	*AR*	NC
5957	r	**V**	H	*VW*	OY

5958 s		H	*VX*	MA
5959 n	**AR**	H	*AR*	NC
5960 s	**V**	H	*VX*	MA
5961 s pt	**V**	H	*VX*	MA
5962 s pt	**V**	H	*VX*	MA
5963 r	**V**	H	*VW*	OY
5964	**AR**	H	*AR*	NC
5965 t		H	*VX*	MA
5966	**AR**	H	*AR*	NC
5967 t	**V**	H	*VX*	MA
5968	**AR**	H	*AR*	NC
5969 u	**V**	H	*VW*	OY
5971 s		H	*VX*	MA
5973	**AR**	H	*AR*	NC
5975 s	**V**	H	*VX*	MA
5976 t	**V**	H	*VX*	MA
5977 r	**V**	H	*VW*	OY
5978 r	**V**	H	*VW*	OY
5980 r	**V**	H	*VW*	OY
5981 s		H	*VX*	MA
5983 s	**V**	H	*VX*	MA
5984 r	**V**	H	*VW*	OY
5985	**AR**	H	*AR*	NC
5986 r	**V**	H	*VW*	OY
5987 r	**V**	H	*VW*	OY
5988 r	**V**	H	*VW*	OY
5989 t	**V**	H	*VX*	MA
5991 s	**V**	H	*VX*	MA
5993 *	**AR**	H	*AR*	NC
5994 r	**V**	H	*VX*	MA
5995 s		H	*VX*	MA
5996 s pt	**V**	H	*VX*	MA
5997 r	**V**	H	*VW*	OY
5998	**AR**	H	*AR*	NC
5999 s	**V**	H	*VX*	MA
6000 t	**V**	H	*VX*	MA
6001 u	**V**	H	*VW*	OY
6002 †	**V**	H	*VW*	OY
6005 r	**V**	H	*VX*	MA
6006	**AR**	H	*AR*	NC
6008 s	**V**	H	*VX*	MA
6009 r	**V**	H	*VW*	OY
6010 s	**V**	H	*VX*	MA
6011 s	**V**	H	*VX*	MA
6012 r	**V**	H	*VW*	OY
6013 s		H	*VX*	MA
6014 s pt		H	*VX*	MA
6015 t	**V**	H	*VX*	MA
6016 r	**V**	H	*VW*	OY
6018 t	**V**	H	*VX*	MA
6021 r	**V**	H	*VW*	OY
6022 s	**V**	H	*VX*	MA
6024 s	**V**	H	*VX*	MA
6025 t	**V**	H	*VX*	MA
6026 s	**V**	H	*VX*	MA
6027 u	**V**	H	*VW*	OY
6028	**AR**	H	*AR*	NC
6029 r	**V**	H	*VW*	OY
6030 t	**V**	H	*VX*	MA
6031 r	**V**	H	*VW*	OY
6034	**AR**	H	*AR*	NC
6035 t		H	*VX*	MA
6036 *	**AR**	H	*AR*	NC
6037	**AR**	H	*AR*	NC
6038 s	**V**	H	*VX*	MA
6041 s	**V**	H	*VX*	MA
6042	**AR**	H	*AR*	NC
6043 †	**V**	H	*VW*	OY
6045 †w	**V**	H	*VW*	OY
6046 s	**V**	H	*VX*	MA
6047 †n*	**V**	H	*VW*	OY
6049 r	**V**	H	*VW*	OY
6050 s		H	*VX*	MA
6051 r	**V**	H	*VW*	OY
6052 tw		H	*VX*	MA
6053 *	**AR**	H	*AR*	NC
6054 r	**V**	H	*VW*	OY
6055 †	**V**	H	*VW*	OY
6056 †	**V**	H	*VW*	OY
6057 r	**V**	H	*VW*	OY
6059 s	**V**	H	*VX*	MA
6060 u	**V**	H	*VW*	OY
6061 s pt	**V**	H	*VX*	MA
6062 †	**V**	H	*VW*	OY
6063 †w	**V**	H	*VW*	OY
6064 s	**V**	H	*VX*	MA
6065 r	**V**	H	*VW*	OY
6066 s		H	*VX*	MA
6067 s pt	**V**	H	*VX*	MA
6073 s	**V**	H	*VX*	MA
6100 †*	**V**	H	*VW*	OY
6101 r	**V**	H	*VW*	OY
6102 r	**V**	H	*VW*	OY
6103	**AR**	H	*AR*	NC
6104 r	**V**	H	*VW*	OY
6105 tpt	**V**	H	*VX*	MA
6106 r	**V**	H	*VW*	OY
6107 r	**V**	H	*VW*	OY
6110		H	*AR*	NC
6111 †	**V**	H	*VW*	OY
6112 s pt	**V**	H	*VX*	MA
6113 †	**V**	H	*VW*	OY

6115	s		H	*VX*	MA
6116	†	**V**	H	*VW*	OY
6117	t	**V**	H	*VX*	MA
6119	s	**V**	H	*VX*	MA
6120	s	**V**	H	*VX*	MA
6121	†	**V**	H	*VW*	OY
6122	s	**V**	H	*VX*	MA
6123		**AR**	H	*AR*	NC
6124	s pt		H	*VX*	MA
6134	†	**V**	H	*VW*	OY
6135	s		H	*VX*	MA
6136	r	**V**	H	*VW*	OY
6137	s pt	**V**	H	*VX*	MA
6138	†	**V**	H	*VW*	OY
6139	n*		H	*AR*	NC
6141	u	**V**	H	*VW*	OY
6142	†*	**V**	H	*VW*	OY
6144	†*	**V**	H	*VW*	OY
6145	s pt	**V**	H	*VX*	MA
6146	*	**AR**	H	*AR*	NC
6147	r	**V**	H	*VW*	OY
6148	s		H	*VX*	MA
6149	u	**V**	H	*VW*	OY
6150	s		H	*VX*	MA
6151	†*	**V**	H	*VW*	OY
6152	*	**AR**	H	*AR*	NC
6153	†	**V**	H	*VW*	OY
6154	r pt		H	*VX*	MA
6155	*	**AR**	H	*AR*	NC
6157	s	**V**	H	*VX*	MA
6158	r	**V**	H	*VW*	OY
6159	s pt	**V**	H	*VX*	MA
6160	*	**AR**	H	*AR*	NC
6161	†*	**V**	H	*VW*	OY
6162	s pt	**V**	H	*VX*	MA
6163	r	**V**	H	*VW*	OY
6164	†	**V**	H	*VW*	OY
6165	r	**V**	H	*VW*	OY
6166			H	*AR*	NC
6167		**AR**	H	*AR*	NC
6168	s		H	*VX*	MA
6170	s	**V**	H	*VX*	MA
6171	†	**V**	H	*VW*	OY
6172	s	**V**	H	*VX*	MA
6173	s	**V**	H	*VX*	MA
6174		**AR**	H	*AR*	NC
6175	r	**V**	H	*VW*	OY
6176	t	**V**	H	*VX*	MA
6177	s	**V**	H	*VX*	MA
6178	s		H	*VX*	MA
6179	r	**V**	H	*VW*	OY
6180	†w	**V**	H	*VW*	OY
6181	†wn	**V**	H	*VW*	OY
6182	s	**V**	H	*VX*	MA
6183	s	**V**	H	*VX*	MA
6184	s	**V**	H	*VX*	MA

AC2D (TSO) OPEN STANDARD

Dia. AC217. Mark 2D. Air conditioned (Stones). Rebuilt from FO with new style 2+2 seats. –/58 2T. (–/58 1T*). B4 bogies. d. ETH 5X.

Lot No. 30821 Derby 1971–72. 33.5 t.

* One toilet converted to store room.

6200	(3198)	**FG**	H	*GW*	OO
6202	(3191)*	**FG**	H	*GW*	OO
6203	(3180)	**FG**	H	*GW*	OO
6206	(3183)	**FG**	H	*GW*	OO
6207	(3204)	**FG**	H	*GW*	OO
6212	(3176)	**FG**	H	*GW*	OO
6213	(3208)	**FG**	H	*GW*	OO
6219	(3213)	**FG**	H	*GW*	OO
6221	(3173)	**FG**	H	*GW*	OO
6226	(3203)	**FG**	H	*GW*	OO

GX51 BRAKE GENERATOR VAN

Dia. GX501. Mark 1. Renumbered 1989 from BR departmental series. Converted from NDA in 1973 to three-phase supply brake generator van for use with HST trailers. Modified 1999 for use with loco-hauled stock. B5 bogies.

Lot No. 30400 Pressed Steel 1958.

6310 (81448, 975325) **CH** RV *SS* CP

AX51 GENERATOR VAN

Dia. AX501. Mark 1. Converted from NDA in 1992 to generator vans for use on Anglo-Scottish sleeping car services. Now normally used on trains hauled by steam locomotives. B4 bogies. ETH75.

6311. Lot No. 30162 Pressed Steel 1958. 37.25 t.
6312. Lot No. 30224 Cravens 1956. 37.25 t.
6313. Lot No. 30484 Pressed Steel 1958. 37.25 t.

6313 is leased to the Venice Simplon Orient Express.

6311	(80903, 92911)		**B**	RS	*SS*	BN
6312	(81023, 92925)		**PC**	FS	*SS*	SZ
6313	(81553, 92167)		**PC**	P	*SS*	SL

GS5 (HSBV) HST BARRIER VEHICLE

Dia. Various diagrams. Renumbered from BR departmental series, or converted from various types. B4 bogies (Commonwealth bogies *).

6330. Mark 2A. Lot No. 30786 Derby 1968. 32 t.
6334. Mark 1. Lot No. 30400 Pressed Steel 1957–8. 31.5 t.
6336/8/44. Mark 1. Lot No. 30715 Gloucester 1962. 31 t.
6340. Mark 1. Lot No. 30669 Swindon 1962. 36 t.
6346. Mark 2A. Lot No. 30777 Derby 1967. 31.5 t.
6348. Mark 1. Lot No. 30163 Pressed Steel 1957. 31.5 t.

Non-standard Livery: 6344 & 6346 are GNER plain dark blue.

6330	(14084, 975629)		**G**	A	*A*	LA
6334	(81478, 92128)		**P**	P	*P*	NL
6336	(81591, 92185)		**G**	A	*A*	LA
6338	(81581, 92180)		**G**	A	*A*	LA
6340	(21251, 975678)	*	**G**	A	*A*	LA
6344	(81263, 92080)		**0**	A	*A*	EC
6346	(9422)		**0**	A	*A*	EC
6348	(81233, 92963)		**G**	A	*A*	LA

GF5 (MFBV) MARK 4 BARRIER VEHICLE

Various diagrams. Converted from FK* or BSO. B4 bogies.

6352/3. Mark 2A. Lot No. 30774 Derby 1968. 33 t.
6354/5. Mark 2C. Lot No. 30820 Derby 1970. 32 t.
6358/9. Mark 2A. Lot No. 30788 Derby 1968. 31.5 t.

Non-standard Livery: GNER plain dark blue.

6352	(13465, 19465)	*	**0**	H	*GN*	BN
6353	(13478, 19478)	*	**0**	H	*GN*	BN
6354	(9459)		**0**	H	*GN*	BN
6355	(9477)		**0**	H	*GN*	BN
6358	(9432)		**0**	H	*GN*	BN

6359	(9429)	**0**	H	*GN*	BN

GF5 (BV) DMU TRANSLATOR VEHICLE

Various diagrams. Mark 2A or 2C. Converted 1992 from BSO.

6360. Mark 2A. Lot No. 30777 Derby 1967. B4 bogies. 31.5 t.
6361. Mark 2C. Lot No. 30820 Derby 1970. B4 bogies. 32 t.

6360	(9420)	**RR**	P	*P*	NL
6361	(9460)	**RR**	P	*P*	NL

GF5 (BV) EMU TRANSLATOR VEHICLE

Various diagrams. Mark 1. Converted 1992 from BG.

6364. Mark 1. Lot No. 30039 Derby 1954. BR Mark 1 bogies. 32 t.
6365. Mark 1. Lot No. 30323 Pressed Steel 1957. BR Mark 1 bogies. 32 t.

6364	(80565)	**RR**	P	*P*	TS
6365	(81296, 84296)	**RR**	P	*P*	TS

GS5 (HSBV) HST BARRIER VEHICLE

Dia. GS507. Mark 1. Converted from BG in 1994–5. B4 bogies.

6392. Lot No. 30715 Gloucester 1962. 29.5 t.
6393/6/7. Lot No. 30716 Gloucester 1962. 29.5 t.
6394. Lot No. 30162 Pressed Steel 1956–57. 30.5 t.
6395. Lot No. 30484 Pressed Steel 1958. 30.5 t.
6398/9. Lot No. 30400 Pressed Steel 1957–58. 30.5 t.

6392	(81588, 92183)	**P**	P	*P*	LA
6393	(81609, 92196)	**P**	P	*P*	LA
6394	(80878, 92906)	**P**	P	*P*	NL
6395	(81506, 92148)	**P**	P	*P*	NL
6396	(81606, 92195)	**P**	P	*P*	LA
6397	(81600, 92190)	**P**	P	*P*	NL
6398	(81471, 92126)	**P**	P	*P*	NL
6399	(81367, 92994)	**P**	P	*P*	NL

AG2C (TSOT) OPEN STANDARD (TROLLEY)

Dia. AG201. Mark 2C. Converted from TSO by removal of one seating bay and replacing this by a counter with a space for a trolley. Adjacent toilet removed and converted to steward's washing area/store. Pressure ventilated. –/54 1T. B4 bogies. ETH 4.

Lot No. 30795 Derby 1969–70. 32.5 t.

6528	(5592)	**M**	WC	*SS*	CS

AG2D (TSOT) OPEN STANDARD (TROLLEY)

Dia. AG202. Mark 2D. Converted from TSO by removal of one seating bay and replacing this by a counter with a space for a trolley. Adjacent toilet removed and converted to steward's washing area/store. Air conditioned. Stones equipment. –/54 1T. B4 bogies. ETH 5.

Lot No. 30822 Derby 1971. 33 t.

6609	(5698)	H	KT
6619	(5655)	H	KT

AN1F (RLO) SLEEPER RECEPTION CAR

Dia. AN101 (AN102*). Mark 2F. Converted from FO, these vehicles consist of pantry, microwave cooking facilities, seating area for passengers, telephone booth and staff toilet. 6703–8 also have a bar. Converted at RTC, Derby (6700), Ilford (6701–5) and Derby (6706–8). Air conditioned. 6700/1/3/5/–8 have Stones equipment and 6702/4 have Temperature Ltd. equipment. 26/– 1T. B4 bogies. p. q. d. ETH 5X.

6700–2/4/8. Lot No. 30859 Derby 1973–74. 33.5 t.
6703/5–7. Lot No. 30845 Derby 1973. 33.5 t.

6700	(3347)		**CS**	H	*SR*	IS
6701	(3346)	*	**CS**	H	*SR*	IS
6702	(3421)	*	**CS**	H	*SR*	IS
6703	(3308)		**CS**	H	*SR*	IS
6704	(3341)		**CS**	H	*SR*	IS
6705	(3310, 6430)		**CS**	H	*SR*	IS
6706	(3283, 6421)		**CS**	H	*SR*	IS
6707	(3276, 6418)		**CS**	H	*SR*	IS
6708	(3370)		**CS**	H	*SR*	IS

AN1D (RMBF) MINIATURE BUFFET CAR

Dia. AN103. Mark 2D. Converted from TSOT by the removal of another seating bay and fitting a proper buffet counter with boiler and microwave oven. Now converted to first class with new seating and end luggage stacks. Air conditioned. Stones equipment. 30/– 1T. B4 bogies. p. q. d. ETH 5.

Lot No. 30822 Derby 1971. 33 t.

6720	(5622, 6652)	**FG**	H	*GW*	OO
6721	(5627, 6660)	**FG**	H	*GW*	OO
6722	(5736, 6661)	**FG**	H	*GW*	OO
6723	(5641, 6662)	**FG**	H	*GW*	OO
6724	(5721, 6665)	**FG**	H	*GW*	OO

AC2F (TSO) OPEN STANDARD

Dia. AC224. Mark 2F. Renumbered from FO and declassified in 1985–6. Converted 1990 to TSO with mainly unidirectional seating and power-operated sliding doors. Air conditioned. 6800–14 were converted by BREL Derby and have Temperature Ltd. air conditioning. 6815–29 were converted by RFS Industries Doncaster and have Stones air conditioning. –/74 2T. B4 bogies. d. ETH 5X.

6800–07. 6810–12. 6813–14. 6819/22/28. Lot No. 30859 Derby 1973–74. 33 t.
6808–6809. Lot No. 30873 Derby 1974–75. 33.5 t.
6815–18. 6820–21. 6823–27. 6829. Lot No. 30845 Derby 1973. 33 t.

6800	(3323, 6435)	**AR**	H	*AR*	NC
6801	(3349, 6442)	**AR**	H	*AR*	NC
6802	(3339, 6439)	**AR**	H	*AR*	NC
6803	(3355, 6443)	**AR**	H	*AR*	NC
6804	(3396, 6449)		H	*AR*	NC
6805	(3324, 6436)	**AR**	H	*AR*	NC
6806	(3342, 6440)	**AR**	H	*AR*	NC
6807	(3423, 6452)		H	*AR*	NC
6808	(3430, 6454)	**AR**	H	*AR*	NC
6809	(3435, 6455)	**AR**	H	*AR*	NC
6810	(3404, 6451)	**AR**	H	*AR*	NC
6811	(3327, 6437)	**AR**	H	*AR*	NC
6812	(3394, 6448)	**AR**	H	*AR*	NC
6813	(3410, 6463)		H	*AR*	NC
6814	(3422, 6465)	**AR**	H	*AR*	NC
6815	(3282, 6420)	**AR**	H	*AR*	NC
6816	(3316, 6461)	**AR**	H	*AR*	NC
6817	(3311, 6431)	**AR**	H	*AR*	NC
6818	(3298, 6427)	**AR**	H	*AR*	NC
6819	(3365, 6446)	**AR**	H	*AR*	NC
6820	(3320, 6434)	**AR**	H	*AR*	NC
6821	(3281, 6458)	**AR**	H	*AR*	NC
6822	(3376, 6447)	**AR**	H	*AR*	NC
6823	(3289, 6424)	**AR**	H	*AR*	NC
6824	(3307, 6429)	**AR**	H	*AR*	NC
6825	(3301, 6460)	**AR**	H	*AR*	NC
6826	(3294, 6425)	**AR**	H	*AR*	NC
6827	(3306, 6428)	**AR**	H	*AR*	NC
6828	(3380, 6464)	**AR**	H	*AR*	NC
6829	(3288, 6423)	**AR**	H	*AR*	NC

NM51 MERSEYRAIL SANDITE COACH

Dia. NM504. Mark 1. Former Class 501 750 V d.c. third rail EMU driving trailers converted for use as Sandite/de-icing coaches. BR Mark 1 Bogies.

Lot No. 30328 Eastleigh 1958. 30 5. t.

6910	(75178, 977346)	**MS**	RK	*RK*	BD
6911	(75180, 977348)	**MS**	RK	*RK*	BD

AH2Z (BSOT) OPEN BRAKE STANDARD (MICRO-BUFFET)

Dia. AH203. Mark 2. Converted from BSO by removal of one seating bay and replacing this by a counter with a space for a trolley. Adjacent toilet removed and converted to a steward's washing area/store. –/23 0T. B4 bogies. ETH 4.

Lot No. 30757 Derby 1966. 31 t.

9100	(9405)	v	**RR**	H		LT
9101	(9398)	v	**RR**	H		TM
9104	(9401)	v	**G**	MH	*SS*	RL

AE21 (BSO) OPEN BRAKE STANDARD

Dia. AE201. Mark 1. –/39 1T. BR Mark 1 bogies. ETH 3.

Lot No. 30170 Doncaster 1955–56. 34 t.

9274 v **CH** NY *SS* NY

AE2Z (BSO) OPEN BRAKE STANDARD

Dia. AE203. Mark 2. These vehicles use the same body shell as the Mark 2 BFK and have first class seat spacing and wider tables. Pressure ventilated. –/31 1T. B4 bogies. ETH 4.

Lot No. 30757 Derby 1966. 31.5 t.

9385 v **LN** H LT
9388 v **LN** H LT
9392 v **G** MH *SS* RL

AE2A (BSO) OPEN BRAKE STANDARD

Dia. AE204. Mark 2A. These vehicles use the same body shell as the Mark 2A BFK and have first class seat spacing and wider tables. Pressure ventilated. –/31 1T. B4 bogies. ETH 4.

9417–21. Lot No. 30777 Derby 1970. 31.5 t.
9428–35. Lot No. 30820 Derby 1970. 31.5 t.

9417 **RB** RV *SS* CP
9421 **RR** H PY
9428 **DR** DR *DR* KM
9434 **RR** H ZN
9435 **RR** H KT

AE2C (BSO) OPEN BRAKE STANDARD

Dia. AE205. Mark 2C. Pressure ventilated. –/31 1T. B4 bogies. ETH 4.

Lot No. 30798 Derby 1970. 32 t.

9440 d **M** WC *VL* CF
9448 d **M** WC *VL* CF

AE2D (BSO) OPEN BRAKE STANDARD

Dia. AE206. Mark 2D. Air conditioned (Stones). –/31 1T. B4 bogies. pg. ETH 5.

r Refurbished with new interior panelling.
s Refurbished with new seating –/22 1TD.
w Facelifted –/28 1W 1T.

Lot No. 30824 Derby 1971. 33 t.

9479	dr		H	*VX*	MA	9488	ds	**FG**	H	*GW*	OO
9480	d	**FG**	H	*GW*	OO	9489	dr	**V**	H	*VX*	MA
9481	ds	**FG**	H	*GW*	OO	9490	ds	**FG**	H	*GW*	OO
9483			H		PY	9492	dw	**FG**	H	*GW*	OO
9484	d		H		CQ	9493	ds	**FG**	H	*GW*	OO
9486			H		PY	9494	ds	**FG**	H	*GW*	OO

AE2E (BSO) OPEN BRAKE STANDARD

Dia. AE207. Mark 2E. Air conditioned (Stones). –/32 1T. B4 bogies. d. pg. ETH 5.

Lot No. 30838 Derby 1972. 33 t.

r Refurbished with new interior panelling.
s Refurbished with modified design of seat headrest and new interior panelling.
w Facelifted –/28 1W 1T.

9496	r		H	*VX*	MA	9504	s	**V**	H	*VX*	MA
9497	r		H	*VX*	MA	9505	s		H	*VX*	MA
9498	r	**V**	H	*VX*	MA	9506	s	**V**	H	*VX*	MA
9500	r		H	*VX*	MA	9507	s	**V**	H	*VX*	MA
9501	w	**FG**	H	*GW*	OO	9508	s	**V**	H	*VX*	MA
9502	s	**V**	H	*VX*	MA	9509	s	**V**	H	*VX*	MA
9503	s	**V**	H	*VX*	MA						

AE2F (BSO) OPEN BRAKE STANDARD

Dia. AE208. Mark 2F. Air conditioned (Temperature Ltd.). All now refurbished with power-operated vestibule doors, new panels and seat trim. All now further refurbished with carpets and new m.a. sets. –/32 1T. B4 bogies. d. pg. ETH5X.

Lot No. 30861 Derby 1974. 34 t.

9513		**V**	H	*VX*	MA	9526	n		H	*VX*	MA
9516	n	**V**	H	*VX*	MA	9527	n	**V**	H	*VX*	MA
9520	n	**V**	H	*VX*	MA	9529	n	**V**	H	*VX*	MA
9521		**V**	H	*VX*	MA	9531		**V**	H	*VX*	MA
9522		**V**	H	*VX*	MA	9537	n	**V**	H	*VX*	MA
9523		**V**	H	*VX*	MA	9538		**V**	H	*VX*	MA
9524	n	**V**	H	*VX*	MA	9539		**V**	H	*VX*	MA
9525		**V**	H	*VX*	MA						

AF2F (DBSO) DRIVING OPEN BRAKE STANDARD

Dia. AF201. Mark 2F. Air conditioned (Temperature Ltd.). Push & pull (t.d.m. system). Converted from BSO, these vehicles originally had half cabs at the brake end. They have since been refurbished and have had their cabs widened and the cab-end gangways removed. –/30 1W 1T. B4 bogies. d. pg. Cowcatchers. ETH 5X.

9701–9710. Lot No. 30861 Derby 1974. Converted Glasgow 1979. Disc brakes. 34 t.
9711–9713. Lot No. 30861 Derby 1974. Converted Glasgow 1985. 34 t.

9714. Lot No. 30861 Derby 1974. Converted Glasgow 1986. Disc brakes. 34 t.

9701	(9528)	**AR**	H	*AR*	NC
9702	(9510)	**AR**	H	*AR*	NC
9703	(9517)	**AR**	H	*AR*	NC
9704	(9512)	**AR**	H	*AR*	NC
9705	(9519)	**AR**	H	*AR*	NC
9707	(9511)	**AR**	H	*AR*	NC
9708	(9530)	**AR**	H	*AR*	NC
9709	(9515)	**AR**	H	*AR*	NC
9710	(9518)		H	*AR*	NC
9711	(9532)	**AR**	H	*AR*	NC
9712	(9534)	**AR**	H	*AR*	NC
9713	(9535)	**AR**	H	*AR*	NC
9714	(9536)	**AR**	H	*AR*	NC

AE4E (BUO) UNCLASSIFIED OPEN BRAKE

Dia. AE401. Mark 2E. Converted from TSO with new seating for use on Anglo-Scottish overnight services by Railcare, Wolverton. Air conditioned. Stones equipment. B4 bogies. d. –/31 1T. B4 bogies. ETH 4X.

9801–9803. Lot No. 30837 Derby 1972. 33.5 t.
9804–9810. Lot No. 30844 Derby 1972–73. 33.5 t.

9800	(5751)	**CS**	H	*SR*	IS
9801	(5760)	**CS**	H	*SR*	IS
9802	(5772)	**CS**	H	*SR*	IS
9803	(5799)	**CS**	H	*SR*	IS
9804	(5826)	**CS**	H	*SR*	IS
9805	(5833)	**CS**	H	*SR*	IS
9806	(5840)	**CS**	H	*SR*	IS
9807	(5851)	**CS**	H	*SR*	IS
9808	(5871)	**CS**	H	*SR*	IS
9809	(5890)	**CS**	H	*SR*	IS
9810	(5892)	**CS**	H	*SR*	IS

AJ1G (RFM) RESTAURANT BUFFET FIRST (MODULAR)

Dia. AJ103 (10200/1 are Dia. AJ101). Mark 3A. Air conditioned. Converted from HST TRFKs, RFBs and FOs. Refurbished with table lamps and burgundy seat trim (except *). 18/– plus two seats for staff use (*24/–). BT10 bogies. p. q. d. ETH 14X.

10200–10211. Lot No. 30884 Derby 1977. 39.8 t.
10212–10229. Lot No. 30878 Derby 1975–76. 39.8 t.
10230–10260. Lot No. 30890 Derby 1979. 39.8 t.

10200	(40519)	*		P	*AR*	NC
10201	(40520)		**V**	P	*VW*	OY
10202	(40504)		**V**	P	*VW*	MA
10203	(40506)	*	**AR**	P	*AR*	NC
10204	(40502)		**V**	P	*VW*	MA
10205	(40503)		**V**	P	*VW*	OY
10206	(40507)		**V**	P	*VW*	MA
10207	(40516)		**V**	P	*VW*	PC
10208	(40517)		**V**	P	*VW*	MA
10209	(40508)		**V**	P	*VW*	PC
10210	(40509)		**V**	P	*VW*	PC
10211	(40510)		**V**	P	*VW*	PC
10212	(11049)		**V**	P	*VW*	MA
10213	(11050)		**V**	P	*VW*	MA
10214	(11034)	*	**AR**	P	*AR*	NC
10215	(11032)		**V**	P	*VW*	PC
10216	(11041)	*	**AR**	P	*AR*	NC
10217	(11051)		**V**	P	*VW*	MA
10218	(11053)		**V**	P	*VW*	MA
10219	(11047)		**V**	P	*VW*	PC
10220	(11056)		**V**	P	*VW*	OY
10221	(11012)		**V**	P	*VW*	PC
10222	(11063)		**V**	P	*VW*	MA
10223	(11043)	*	**AR**	P	*AR*	NC
10224	(11062)		**V**	P	*VW*	MA
10225	(11014)		**V**	P	*VW*	OY
10226	(11015)		**V**	P	*VW*	MA
10227	(11057)		**V**	P	*VW*	PC

10228	(11035)	*	**AR**	P	*AR*	NC
10229	(11059)		**V**	P	*VW*	MA
10230	(10021)		**V**	P	*VW*	PC
10231	(10016)		**V**	P	*VW*	OY
10232	(10027)		**V**	P	*VW*	OY
10233	(10013)		**V**	P	*VW*	PC
10234	(10004)		**V**	P	*VW*	PC
10235	(10015)		**V**	P	*VW*	OY
10236	(10018)		**V**	P	*VW*	PC
10237	(10022)		**V**	P	*VW*	MA
10238	(10017)		**V**	P	*VW*	OY
10240	(10003)		**V**	P	*VW*	OY
10241	(10009)	*	**AR**	P	*AR*	NC
10242	(10002)		**V**	P	*VW*	OY
10245	(10019)		**V**	P	*VW*	PC
10246	(10014)		**V**	P	*VW*	PC
10247	(10011)	*	**AR**	P	*AR*	NC
10248	(10005)		**V**	P	*VW*	OY
10249	(10012)		**V**	P	*VW*	PC
10250	(10020)		**V**	P	*VW*	OY
10251	(10024)		**V**	P	*VW*	OY
10252	(10008)		**V**	P	*VW*	OY
10253	(10026)		**V**	P	*VW*	PC
10254	(10006)		**V**	P	*VW*	PC
10255	(10010)		**V**	P	*VW*	OY
10256	(10028)		**V**	P	*VW*	MA
10257	(10007)		**V**	P	*VW*	PC
10258	(10023)		**V**	P	*VW*	MA
10259	(10025)		**V**	P	*VW*	OY
10260	(10001)		**V**	P	*VW*	MA

AJ1J (RFM) RESTAURANT BUFFET FIRST (MODULAR)

Dia. AJ105. Mark 4. Air conditioned. 20/– 1T. BT41 bogies. ETH 6X.

Lot No. 31045 Metro-Cammell 1989 onwards. 45.5 t.

10300	**GN**	H	*GN*	BN
10301	**GN**	H	*GN*	BN
10302	**GN**	H	*GN*	BN
10303	**GN**	H	*GN*	BN
10304	**GN**	H	*GN*	BN
10305	**GN**	H	*GN*	BN
10306	**GN**	H	*GN*	BN
10307	**GN**	H	*GN*	BN
10308	**GN**	H	*GN*	BN
10309	**GN**	H	*GN*	BN
10310	**GN**	H	*GN*	BN
10311	**GN**	H	*GN*	BN
10312	**GN**	H	*GN*	BN
10313	**GN**	H	*GN*	BN
10314	**GN**	H	*GN*	BN
10315	**GN**	H	*GN*	BN
10316	**GN**	H	*GN*	BN
10317	**GN**	H	*GN*	BN
10318	**GN**	H	*GN*	BN
10319	**GN**	H	*GN*	BN
10320	**GN**	H	*GN*	BN
10321	**GN**	H	*GN*	BN
10322	**GN**	H		ZF
10323	**GN**	H	*GN*	BN
10324	**GN**	H	*GN*	BN
10325	**GN**	H	*GN*	BN
10326	**GN**	H	*GN*	BN
10327	**GN**	H		ZC
10328	**GN**	H	*GN*	BN
10329	**GN**	H	*GN*	BN
10330	**GN**	H	*GN*	BN
10331	**GN**	H	*GN*	BN
10332	**GN**	H	*GN*	BN
10333	**GN**	H	*GN*	BN

AU4G (SLEP) SLEEPING CAR WITH PANTRY

Dia. AU401. Mark 3A. Air conditioned. Retention toilets. 12 compartments with a fixed lower berth and a hinged upper berth, plus an attendants compartment. 2T BT10 bogies. ETH 7X.

Lot No. 30960 Derby 1981–83. 41 t.

10500			SA		ZF
10501	d	**CS**	P	*SR*	IS
10502	d	**CS**	P	*SR*	IS
10503			SA		ZF
10504	d	**CS**	P	*SR*	IS
10506	d	**CS**	P	*SR*	IS
10507	d	**CS**	P	*SR*	IS
10508	d	**CS**	P	*SR*	IS
10510	d		P		IS
10513	d	**CS**	P	*SR*	IS

10514			SA	ZF
10515	d		P	IS
10516	d	**CS**	P *SR*	IS
10519	d	**CS**	P *SR*	IS
10520	d	**CS**	P *SR*	IS
10522	d	**CS**	P *SR*	IS
10523	d	**CS**	P *SR*	IS
10526	d	**CS**	P *SR*	IS
10527	d	**CS**	P *SR*	IS
10529	d	**CS**	P *SR*	IS
10530	d		P	MM
10531	d	**CS**	P *SR*	IS
10532	d	**FG**	P *GW*	PZ
10533			P	MM
10534	d	**FG**	P *GW*	PZ
10535	d		P	MM
10536	d		P	KT
10537	d		P	MM
10538	d		P	KT
10539	d		P	KT
10540	d		P	MM
10542	d	**CS**	P *SR*	IS
10543	d	**CS**	P *SR*	IS
10544	d	**CS**	P *SR*	IS
10546			P	MM
10547	d		P	IS
10548	d	**CS**	P *SR*	IS
10549	d		P	MM
10550	d		P	MM
10551	d	**CS**	P *SR*	IS
10553	d	**CS**	P *SR*	IS
10554	d		P	ZD
10555	d		P	KT
10557	d		P	ZD
10559	d		P	KT
10560	d		P	MM
10561	d	**CS**	P *SR*	IS
10562	d	**CS**	P *SR*	IS
10563	d	**FG**	P *GW*	PZ
10565	d	**CS**	P *SR*	IS
10566	d		P	MM
10569	d	**PC**	VS *SS*	SL
10570			P	KT
10571			SA	FP
10572	d		P	MM
10574			RS	OM
10575			SA	ZF
10577		**BG**	P	ZD
10578			P	MM
10579		**BG**	P	KT
10580	d	**CS**	P *SR*	IS
10582	d		P	ZD
10583	d	**FG**	P	ZN
10584	d	**FG**	P *GW*	PZ
10586	d		P	KT
10588	d	**FG**	P *GW*	PZ
10589	d	**FG**	P *GW*	PZ
10590	d	**FG**	P *GW*	PZ
10592			P	KT
10593	d		P	KT
10594	d	**FG**	P *GW*	PZ
10596	d		P	KT
10597	d	**CS**	P *SR*	IS
10598	d	**CS**	P *SR*	IS
10600	d	**CS**	P *SR*	IS
10601	d	**FG**	P *GW*	PZ
10602			P	MM
10604			P	ZD
10605	d	**CS**	P *SR*	IS
10607	d	**CS**	P *SR*	IS
10610	d	**CS**	P *SR*	IS
10612	d	**FG**	P *GW*	PZ
10613	d	**CS**	P *SR*	IS
10614	d	**CS**	P *SR*	IS
10616	d	**FG**	P *GW*	PZ
10617	d	**CS**	P *SR*	IS

AS4G (SLE/SLED*) SLEEPING CAR

Dia. AS403 (AS404*). Mark 3A. Air conditioned. Retention toilets. 13 compartments with a fixed lower berth and a hinged upper berth (* 11 compartments with a fixed lower berth and a hinged upper berth + one compartment for a disabled person). 2T. BT10 bogies. ETH 6X.

Notes:

10664/9/76/7/95/8/721 were sold to the Danish State Railways (DSB) when they were numbered in the UIC system. They have since been purchased by Angel Train Contracts and returned to Britain.

10729 is leased to Venice Simplon-Orient Express.

10734 was originally 2914 and used as a Royal Train staff sleeping car and is Dia. AT531. It has 12 berths and a shower room and is ETH11X.

10646–10732. Lot No. 30961 Derby 1980–84. 43.5 t.
10734. Lot No. 31002 Derby/Wolverton 1985. 42.5 t.

10646	d		RS		OM
10647	d		P		KT
10648	d*	**CS**	P	*SR*	IS
10649	d		P		KT
10650	d*	**CS**	P	*SR*	IS
10651	d		P		ZD
10653	d		P		MM
10654	d		P		MM
10655			SA		ZF
10657			SA		ZF
10658	d		P		KT
10660	d		P		ZD
10662			P		ZD
10663	d		P	*SR*	IS
10664		**DS**	CW		ZN
10666	d*	**CS**	P	*SR*	IS
10668	d		P		MM
10669		**DS**	CW		KT
10675	d	**CS**	P	*SR*	IS
10676		**DS**	CW		MM
10677		**DS**	CW		ZN
10678		**BG**	P		KT
10679		**BG**	P		KT
10680	d*	**CS**	P	*SR*	IS
10682	d		P		ZD
10683	d	**CS**	P	*SR*	IS
10686	d		P		MM
10687	d		P		MM
10688	d	**CS**	P	*SR*	IS
10689	d*	**CS**	P	*SR*	IS
10690	d	**CS**	P	*SR*	IS
10691	d		P		MM
10692	d		P		MM
10693	d	**CS**	P	*SR*	IS
10695		**DS**	CW		ZN
10697	d		P		KT
10698		**DS**	CW		MM
10699	d*	**CS**	P	*SR*	IS
10701	d		P		KT
10702			SA		ZF
10703	d	**CS**	P	*SR*	IS
10704	d		AE	*AE*	ZA
10706	d*	**CS**	P	*SR*	IS
10708	d		P		MM
10709	d		P		MM
10710	d		P		KT
10711	d		P		MM
10712	d		P		MM
10713	d		P		MM
10714	d*	**CS**	P	*SR*	IS
10715	d		P		MM
10716	d		P		ZD
10717	d		P		MM
10718	d*	**CS**	P	*SR*	IS
10719	d*	**CS**	P	*SR*	IS
10720			P		KT
10721		**DS**	CW		ZN
10722	d*	**CS**	P	*SR*	IS
10723	d*	**CS**	P	*SR*	IS
10724			SA		FP
10725			SA		ZF
10726			SA		ZF
10727			SA		ZF
10729		**M**	SA	*SS*	CP
10730	d		P		MM
10731	d		P		KT
10732	d		P		KT
10734		**RP**	CW		ZN

AD1G (FO) OPEN FIRST

Dia. AD108. Mark 3A. Air conditioned. All now refurbished with table lamps and new seat cushions and trim. 48/– 2T (* 48/– 1T 1TD). BT10 bogies. d. ETH 6X.

11005–7 were open composites 11905–7 for a time.

Lot No. 30878 Derby 1975–76. 34.3 t.

11005	**V**	P	*VW*	PC
11006	**V**	P	*VW*	PC

11007	**V**	P	*VW*	PC
11011 *	**V**	P	*VW*	MA
11013	**V**	P	*VW*	PC
11016	**V**	P	*VW*	PC
11017	**V**	P	*VW*	PC
11018	**V**	P	*VW*	MA
11019	**V**	P	*VW*	PC
11020	**V**	P	*VW*	MA
11021	**V**	P	*VW*	PC
11023	**V**	P	*VW*	PC
11024	**V**	P	*VW*	MA
11026	**V**	P	*VW*	MA
11027	**V**	P	*VW*	MA
11028	**V**	P	*VW*	MA
11029	**V**	P	*VW*	MA
11030	**V**	P	*VW*	MA
11031	**V**	P	*VW*	MA
11033	**V**	P	*VW*	PC
11036	**V**	P	*VW*	MA
11037	**V**	P	*VW*	PC
11038	**V**	P	*VW*	PC
11039	**V**	P	*VW*	PC
11040	**V**	P	*VW*	MA
11042	**V**	P	*VW*	MA
11044	**V**	P	*VW*	MA
11045	**V**	P	*VW*	PC
11046	**V**	P	*VW*	PC
11048	**V**	P	*VW*	MA
11052	**V**	P	*VW*	MA
11054	**V**	P	*VW*	PC
11055	**V**	P	*VW*	PC
11058	**V**	P	*VW*	MA
11060	**V**	P	*VW*	PC

AD1H (FO) OPEN FIRST

Dia. AD109. Mark 3B. Air conditioned. Inter-City 80 seats. All now refurbished with table lamps and new seat cushions and trim. 48/– 2T. BT10 bogies. d. ETH 6X.

Lot No. 30982 Derby 1985. 36.5 t.

11064	**V**	P	*VW*	MA
11065	**V**	P	*VW*	PC
11066	**V**	P	*VW*	MA
11067	**V**	P	*VW*	PC
11068	**V**	P	*VW*	MA
11069	**V**	P	*VW*	MA
11070	**V**	P	*VW*	MA
11071	**V**	P	*VW*	PC
11072	**V**	P	*VW*	PC
11073	**V**	P	*VW*	MA
11074	**V**	P	*VW*	MA
11075	**V**	P	*VW*	MA
11076	**V**	P	*VW*	MA
11077	**V**	P	*VW*	MA
11078	**V**	P	*VW*	PC
11079	**V**	P	*VW*	MA
11080	**V**	P	*VW*	MA
11081	**V**	P	*VW*	PC
11082	**V**	P	*VW*	PC
11083 p	**V**	P	*VW*	MA
11084 p	**V**	P	*VW*	MA
11085 p	**V**	P	*VW*	MA
11086 p	**V**	P	*VW*	PC
11087 p	**V**	P	*VW*	MA
11088 p	**V**	P	*VW*	PC
11089 p	**V**	P	*VW*	PC
11090 p	**V**	P	*VW*	MA
11091 p	**V**	P	*VW*	MA
11092 p	**V**	P	*VW*	MA
11093 p	**V**	P	*VW*	PC
11094 p	**V**	P	*VW*	MA
11095 p	**V**	P	*VW*	MA
11096 p	**V**	P	*VW*	PC
11097 p	**V**	P	*VW*	MA
11098 p	**V**	P	*VW*	PC
11099 p	**V**	P	*VW*	PC
11100 p	**V**	P	*VW*	PC
11101 p	**V**	P	*VW*	MA

AD1J (FO) OPEN FIRST

Dia. AD111. Mark 4. Air conditioned. 46/– 1T. BT41 bogies. ETH 6X.

11264–71 were cancelled.

Lot No. 31046 Metro-Cammell 1989–92. 39.7 t.

11200		**GN**	H	*GN*	BN
11201	p	**GN**	H	*GN*	BN
11202		**GN**	H	*GN*	BN
11203	p	**GN**	H	*GN*	BN
11204	p	**GN**	H	*GN*	BN
11205		**GN**	H	*GN*	BN
11206		**GN**	H	*GN*	BN
11207	p	**GN**	H	*GN*	BN
11208		**GN**	H	*GN*	BN
11209		**GN**	H	*GN*	BN
11210		**GN**	H	*GN*	BN
11211	p	**GN**	H	*GN*	BN
11212		**GN**	H	*GN*	BN
11213	p	**GN**	H		ZF
11214	p	**GN**	H	*GN*	BN
11215		**GN**	H	*GN*	BN
11216		**GN**	H	*GN*	BN
11217	p	**GN**	H	*GN*	BN
11218		**GN**	H	*GN*	BN
11219	p	**GN**	H	*GN*	BN
11220		**GN**	H	*GN*	BN
11221	p	**GN**	H	*GN*	BN
11222	p	**GN**	H	*GN*	BN
11223		**GN**	H	*GN*	BN
11224		**GN**	H		ZF
11225	p	**GN**	H	*GN*	BN
11226		**GN**	H	*GN*	BN
11227	p	**GN**	H	*GN*	BN
11228	p	**GN**	H	*GN*	BN
11229	p	**GN**	H	*GN*	BN
11230		**GN**	H	*GN*	BN
11231	p	**GN**	H	*GN*	BN
11232		**GN**	H	*GN*	BN
11233	p	**GN**	H	*GN*	BN
11234		**GN**	H	*GN*	BN
11235	p	**GN**	H	*GN*	BN
11236		**GN**	H	*GN*	BN
11237	p	**GN**	H	*GN*	BN
11238		**GN**	H	*GN*	BN
11239	p	**GN**	H	*GN*	BN
11240		**GN**	H	*GN*	BN
11241		**GN**	H	*GN*	BN
11242	p	**GN**	H	*GN*	BN
11243	p	**GN**	H	*GN*	BN
11244		**GN**	H	*GN*	BN
11245	p	**GN**	H	*GN*	BN
11246	p	**GN**	H	*GN*	BN
11247	p	**GN**	H	*GN*	BN
11248		**GN**	H		ZC
11249	p	**GN**	H		ZC
11250		**GN**	H	*GN*	BN
11251	p	**GN**	H	*GN*	BN
11252		**GN**	H	*GN*	BN
11253	p	**GN**	H	*GN*	BN
11254		**GN**	H	*GN*	BN
11255	p	**GN**	H	*GN*	BN
11256		**GN**	H	*GN*	BN
11257	p	**GN**	H	*GN*	BN
11258		**GN**	H	*GN*	BN
11259	p	**GN**	H	*GN*	BN
11260		**GN**	H	*GN*	BN
11261	p	**GN**	H	*GN*	BN
11262		**GN**	H	*GN*	BN
11263	p	**GN**	H	*GN*	BN
11272		**GN**	H	*GN*	BN
11273		**GN**	H	*GN*	BN
11274		**GN**	H	*GN*	BN
11275		**GN**	H	*GN*	BN
11276		**GN**	H	*GN*	BN

AC2G (TSO) OPEN STANDARD

Dia. AC213 (AC220 z). Mark 3A. Air conditioned. All refurbished with modified seat backs and new layout and now further refurbished with new seat trim. –/76 2T (s –/70 2T 2W, z –/70 1TD 1T 2W). BT10 (* BREL T4) bogies. d. ETH 6X.

Note: 12169–72 were converted from open composites 11908–10/22, formerly FOs 11008–10/22.

Lot No. 30877 Derby 1975–77. 34.3 t.

12004	**V**	P	*VW*	MA
12005	**V**	P	*VW*	PC
12007	**V**	P	*VW*	MA
12008	**V**	P	*VW*	MA
12009	**V**	P	*VW*	MA
12010	**V**	P	*VW*	MA
12011	**V**	P	*VW*	PC
12012	**V**	P	*VW*	PC
12013	**V**	P	*VW*	MA
12014	**V**	P	*VW*	PC

12015		V	P	*VW*	PC
12016		V	P	*VW*	PC
12017		V	P	*VW*	MA
12019		V	P	*VW*	PC
12020		V	P	*VW*	PC
12021		V	P	*VW*	PC
12022		V	P	*VW*	MA
12023		V	P	*VW*	PC
12024	s	V	P	*VW*	PC
12025		V	P	*VW*	MA
12026		V	P	*VW*	PC
12027		V	P	*VW*	MA
12028		V	P	*VW*	MA
12029		V	P	*VW*	MA
12030		V	P	*VW*	PC
12031		V	P	*VW*	PC
12032		V	P	*VW*	PC
12033	z	V	P	*VW*	MA
12034		V	P	*VW*	MA
12035		V	P	*VW*	PC
12036	s	V	P	*VW*	PC
12037		V	P	*VW*	PC
12038		V	P	*VW*	PC
12040		V	P	*VW*	PC
12041		V	P	*VW*	PC
12042	s	V	P	*VW*	PC
12043		V	P	*VW*	MA
12044		V	P	*VW*	MA
12045		V	P	*VW*	MA
12046		V	P	*VW*	PC
12047	z	V	P	*VW*	PC
12048		V	P	*VW*	PC
12049		V	P	*VW*	PC
12050	s	V	P	*VW*	PC
12051		V	P	*VW*	PC
12052		V	P	*VW*	MA
12053		V	P	*VW*	MA
12054	s	V	P	*VW*	MA
12055		V	P	*VW*	PC
12056		V	P	*VW*	PC
12057		V	P	*VW*	MA
12058		V	P	*VW*	PC
12059	s	V	P	*VW*	MA
12060		V	P	*VW*	PC
12061	s	V	P	*VW*	PC
12062		V	P	*VW*	PC
12063		V	P	*VW*	MA
12064		V	P	*VW*	PC
12065		V	P	*VW*	MA
12066		V	P	*VW*	MA
12067		V	P	*VW*	MA
12068		V	P	*VW*	MA
12069		V	P	*VW*	MA
12070		V	P	*VW*	PC
12071		V	P	*VW*	PC
12072		V	P	*VW*	MA
12073		V	P	*VW*	MA
12075		V	P	*VW*	PC
12076		V	P	*VW*	PC
12077		V	P	*VW*	PC
12078		V	P	*VW*	MA
12079		V	P	*VW*	PC
12080		V	P	*VW*	PC
12081		V	P	*VW*	PC
12082		V	P	*VW*	PC
12083		V	P	*VW*	MA
12084		V	P	*VW*	MA
12085	s	V	P	*VW*	MA
12086	s	V	P	*VW*	MA
12087	s	V	P	*VW*	PC
12088	z	V	P	*VW*	PC
12089		V	P	*VW*	MA
12090		V	P	*VW*	MA
12091		V	P	*VW*	PC
12092		V	P	*VW*	MA
12093		V	P	*VW*	PC
12094		V	P	*VW*	PC
12095		V	P	*VW*	MA
12096		V	P	*VW*	PC
12097		V	P	*VW*	PC
12098		V	P	*VW*	MA
12099		V	P	*VW*	PC
12100	z	V	P	*VW*	PC
12101	s	V	P	*VW*	PC
12102		V	P	*VW*	PC
12103	s	V	P	*VW*	MA
12104		V	P	*VW*	MA
12105		V	P	*VW*	PC
12106		V	P	*VW*	MA
12107		V	P	*VW*	PC
12108	s	V	P	*VW*	MA
12109	s	V	P	*VW*	MA
12110		V	P	*VW*	MA
12111		V	P	*VW*	MA
12112	z	V	P	*VW*	MA
12113		V	P	*VW*	MA
12114		V	P	*VW*	PC
12115		V	P	*VW*	MA
12116		V	P	*VW*	PC
12117		V	P	*VW*	MA
12118		V	P	*VW*	MA
12119		V	P	*VW*	MA

12120		**V**	P *VW*	MA
12121		**V**	P *VW*	PC
12122	z	**V**	P *VW*	MA
12123		**V**	P *VW*	PC
12124		**V**	P *VW*	MA
12125		**V**	P *VW*	MA
12126		**V**	P *VW*	MA
12127		**V**	P *VW*	PC
12128	s	**V**	P *VW*	MA
12129		**V**	P *VW*	MA
12130		**V**	P *VW*	MA
12131		**V**	P *VW*	PC
12132		**V**	P *VW*	MA
12133		**V**	P *VW*	MA
12134		**V**	P *VW*	PC
12135		**V**	P *VW*	PC
12136		**V**	P *VW*	PC
12137		**V**	P *VW*	PC
12138		**V**	P *VW*	PC
12139		**V**	P *VW*	MA
12140	z*	**V**	P *VW*	PC
12141		**V**	P *VW*	PC
12142	z	**V**	P *VW*	PC
12143		**V**	P *VW*	PC
12144	s	**V**	P *VW*	PC
12145		**V**	P *VW*	MA
12146		**V**	P *VW*	PC
12147		**V**	P *VW*	PC
12148		**V**	P *VW*	PC
12149		**V**	P *VW*	PC
12150		**V**	P *VW*	PC
12151		**V**	P *VW*	PC
12152		**V**	P *VW*	PC
12153		**V**	P *VW*	PC
12154		**V**	P *VW*	MA
12155	s	**V**	P *VW*	PC
12156		**V**	P *VW*	MA
12157		**V**	P *VW*	MA
12158		**V**	P *VW*	PC
12159		**V**	P *VW*	PC
12160	s	**V**	P *VW*	PC
12161	z	**V**	P *VW*	MA
12163		**V**	P *VW*	MA
12164		**V**	P *VW*	PC
12165		**V**	P *VW*	MA
12166		**V**	P *VW*	PC
12167		**V**	P *VW*	PC
12168	s	**V**	P *VW*	PC
12169	s	**V**	P *VW*	MA
12170	s	**V**	P *VW*	MA
12171	s	**V**	P *VW*	PC
12172	s	**V**	P *VW*	PC

AI2J (TSOE) OPEN STANDARD (END)

Dia. AI201. Mark 4. Air conditioned. –/74 2T. BT41 bogies. ETH 6X.

Lot No. 31047 Metro-Cammell 1989–91. 39.5 t.

12232 was converted from the original 12405.

12200	**GN**	H *GN*	BN
12201	**GN**	H *GN*	BN
12202	**GN**	H *GN*	BN
12203	**GN**	H *GN*	BN
12204	**GN**	H *GN*	BN
12205	**GN**	H *GN*	BN
12206	**GN**	H	ZF
12207	**GN**	H *GN*	BN
12208	**GN**	H *GN*	BN
12209	**GN**	H *GN*	BN
12210	**GN**	H *GN*	BN
12211	**GN**	H *GN*	BN
12212	**GN**	H *GN*	BN
12213	**GN**	H *GN*	BN
12214	**GN**	H *GN*	BN
12215	**GN**	H *GN*	BN
12216	**GN**	H *GN*	BN
12217	**GN**	H	ZC
12218	**GN**	H *GN*	BN
12219	**GN**	H *GN*	BN
12220	**GN**	H *GN*	BN
12222	**GN**	H *GN*	BN
12223	**GN**	H *GN*	BN
12224	**GN**	H *GN*	BN
12225	**GN**	H *GN*	BN
12226	**GN**	H *GN*	BN
12227	**GN**	H *GN*	BN
12228	**GN**	H *GN*	BN
12229	**GN**	H *GN*	BN
12230	**GN**	H *GN*	BN
12231	**GN**	H *GN*	BN
12232	**GN**	H *GN*	BN

AL2J (TSOD) OPEN STANDARD (DISABLED ACCESS)

Dia. AL201. Mark 4. Air conditioned. –/72 1TD 1W. BT41 bogies. p. ETH 6X.

Lot No. 31048 Metro-Cammell 1989–91. 39.4 t.

12300	**GN**	H	*GN*	BN
12301	**GN**	H	*GN*	BN
12302	**GN**	H	*GN*	BN
12303	**GN**	H	*GN*	BN
12304	**GN**	H	*GN*	BN
12305	**GN**	H	*GN*	BN
12306	**GN**	H		ZF
12307	**GN**	H	*GN*	BN
12308	**GN**	H	*GN*	BN
12309	**GN**	H	*GN*	BN
12310	**GN**	H	*GN*	BN
12311	**GN**	H	*GN*	BN
12312	**GN**	H	*GN*	BN
12313	**GN**	H	*GN*	BN
12314	**GN**	H		ZC
12315	**GN**	H	*GN*	BN
12316	**GN**	H	*GN*	BN
12317	**GN**	H	*GN*	BN
12318	**GN**	H	*GN*	BN
12319	**GN**	H	*GN*	BN
12320	**GN**	H	*GN*	BN
12321	**GN**	H	*GN*	BN
12322	**GN**	H	*GN*	BN
12323	**GN**	H	*GN*	BN
12324	**GN**	H	*GN*	BN
12325	**GN**	H	*GN*	BN
12326	**GN**	H	*GN*	BN
12327	**GN**	H	*GN*	BN
12328	**GN**	H	*GN*	BN
12329	**GN**	H	*GN*	BN
12330	**GN**	H	*GN*	BN

AC2J (TSO) OPEN STANDARD

Dia. AC214. Mark 4. Air conditioned. –/74 2T. BT41 bogies. ETH 6X.

Lot No. 31049 Metro-Cammell 1989–92. 39.9 t.

12405 is the second coach to carry that number. It was built from the bodyshell originally intended for 12221. The original 12405 is now 12232. 12490–12512 were cancelled.

12400	**GN**	H	*GN*	BN
12401	**GN**	H	*GN*	BN
12402	**GN**	H	*GN*	BN
12403	**GN**	H	*GN*	BN
12404	**GN**	H	*GN*	BN
12405	**GN**	H	*GN*	BN
12406	**GN**	H	*GN*	BN
12407	**GN**	H	*GN*	BN
12408	**GN**	H	*GN*	BN
12409	**GN**	H	*GN*	BN
12410	**GN**	H	*GN*	BN
12411	**GN**	H	*GN*	BN
12412	**GN**	H		ZF
12413	**GN**	H		ZF
12414	**GN**	H	*GN*	BN
12415	**GN**	H	*GN*	BN
12416	**GN**	H	*GN*	BN
12417	**GN**	H	*GN*	BN
12418	**GN**	H	*GN*	BN
12419	**GN**	H	*GN*	BN
12420	**GN**	H	*GN*	BN
12421	**GN**	H	*GN*	BN
12422	**GN**	H	*GN*	BN
12423	**GN**	H	*GN*	BN
12424	**GN**	H	*GN*	BN
12425	**GN**	H	*GN*	BN
12426	**GN**	H	*GN*	BN
12427	**GN**	H	*GN*	BN
12428	**GN**	H	*GN*	BN
12429	**GN**	H	*GN*	BN
12430	**GN**	H	*GN*	BN
12431	**GN**	H	*GN*	BN
12432	**GN**	H	*GN*	BN
12433	**GN**	H	*GN*	BN
12434	**GN**	H	*GN*	BN
12435	**GN**	H	*GN*	BN
12436	**GN**	H	*GN*	BN
12437	**GN**	H	*GN*	BN

12438	**GN**	H		ZC
12439	**GN**	H	*GN*	BN
12440	**GN**	H	*GN*	BN
12441	**GN**	H	*GN*	BN
12442	**GN**	H	*GN*	BN
12443	**GN**	H	*GN*	BN
12444	**GN**	H	*GN*	BN
12445	**GN**	H	*GN*	BN
12446	**GN**	H	*GN*	BN
12447	**GN**	H	*GN*	BN
12448	**GN**	H	*GN*	BN
12449	**GN**	H	*GN*	BN
12450	**GN**	H	*GN*	BN
12451	**GN**	H	*GN*	BN
12452	**GN**	H	*GN*	BN
12453	**GN**	H	*GN*	BN
12454	**GN**	H	*GN*	BN
12455	**GN**	H	*GN*	BN
12456	**GN**	H	*GN*	BN
12457	**GN**	H	*GN*	BN
12458	**GN**	H	*GN*	BN
12459	**GN**	H	*GN*	BN
12460	**GN**	H	*GN*	BN
12461	**GN**	H	*GN*	BN
12462	**GN**	H	*GN*	BN
12463	**GN**	H	*GN*	BN
12464	**GN**	H	*GN*	BN
12465	**GN**	H	*GN*	BN
12466	**GN**	H	*GN*	BN
12467	**GN**	H	*GN*	BN
12468	**GN**	H	*GN*	BN
12469	**GN**	H	*GN*	BN
12470	**GN**	H	*GN*	BN
12471	**GN**	H		ZC
12472	**GN**	H	*GN*	BN
12473	**GN**	H	*GN*	BN
12474	**GN**	H	*GN*	BN
12475	**GN**	H	*GN*	BN
12476	**GN**	H	*GN*	BN
12477	**GN**	H	*GN*	BN
12478	**GN**	H	*GN*	BN
12479	**GN**	H	*GN*	BN
12480	**GN**	H	*GN*	BN
12481	**GN**	H	*GN*	BN
12482	**GN**	H	*GN*	BN
12483	**GN**	H	*GN*	BN
12484	**GN**	H	*GN*	BN
12485	**GN**	H	*GN*	BN
12486	**GN**	H	*GN*	BN
12487	**GN**	H	*GN*	BN
12488	**GN**	H	*GN*	BN
12489	**GN**	H	*GN*	BN
12513	**GN**	H	*GN*	BN
12514	**GN**	H	*GN*	BN
12515	**GN**	H	*GN*	BN
12516	**GN**	H		ZF
12517	**GN**	H		ZC
12518	**GN**	H	*GN*	BN
12519	**GN**	H	*GN*	BN
12520	**GN**	H	*GN*	BN
12521	**GN**	H	*GN*	BN
12522	**GN**	H	*GN*	BN
12523	**GN**	H	*GN*	BN
12524	**GN**	H	*GN*	BN
12525	**GN**	H		ZF
12526	**GN**	H	*GN*	BN
12527	**GN**	H	*GN*	BN
12528	**GN**	H	*GN*	BN
12529	**GN**	H	*GN*	BN
12530	**GN**	H	*GN*	BN
12531	**GN**	H		ZC
12532	**GN**	H	*GN*	BN
12533	**GN**	H	*GN*	BN
12534	**GN**	H	*GN*	BN
12535	**GN**	H	*GN*	BN
12536	**GN**	H	*GN*	BN
12537	**GN**	H	*GN*	BN
12538	**GN**	H	*GN*	BN

AA11 (FK) CORRIDOR FIRST

Dia. AA101. Mark 1. 42/– 2T. ETH 3.

13225–13230. Lot No. 30381 Swindon 1959. B4 bogies. 33 t.
13318–13341. Lot No. 30667 Swindon 1962. Commonwealth bogies. 36 t.

f Fitted with fluorescent lighting.

13225	k	**RR**	H		EC
13227	xk	**CH**	RV	*SS*	CP
13229	xk	**M**	BK	*SS*	BT
13230	xk	**M**	BK	*SS*	BT
13318			SO	*SO*	ZA
13321	x	**M**	WC	*SS*	CS

13341	f	**WR**	SO	*SO*	ZA				

AA1A (FK) CORRIDOR FIRST

Dia. AA106. Mark 2A. Pressure ventilated. 42/– 2T. B4 bogies. ETH 4.

13440. Lot No. 30774 Derby 1968. 33 t.
13474. Lot No. 30785 Derby 1968. 33 t.

13440	v	**G**	MH	*SS*	RL	13474	v	**G**	MH	*SS*	RL

AA1D (FK) CORRIDOR FIRST

Dia. AA109. Mark 2D. Air conditioned (Stones). 42/– 2T. B4 bogies. ETH 5.

Lot No. 30825 Derby 1971–72. 34.5 t.

13582	E	KT	13604	RS	FP
13585	RV	CP	13607	RS	FP

AB11 (BFK) CORRIDOR BRAKE FIRST

Dia. AB101. Mark 1. 24/– 1T. Commonwealth bogies. ETH 2.

17007. Lot No. 30382 Swindon 1959. 35 t.
17013–17019. Lot No. 30668 Swindon 1961. 36 t.
17023. Lot No. 30718 Swindon 1963. Metal window frames. 36 t.

Originally numbered 14007/13/15/18/19/23.

17007	x	**PC**	MN	*OS*	SL	17018	v	**CH**	VT	*SS*	TM
17013		**PC**	FS	*OS*	SZ	17019	x	**M**	NE	*OS*	BQ
17015	x	**G**	RS	*SS*	BN	17023	x	**G**	RS	*SS*	BN

AB1A (BFK) CORRIDOR BRAKE FIRST

Dia. AB103. Mark 2A. Pressure ventilated. 24/– 1T. B4 bogies. ETH 4.

17056–17077. Lot No. 30775 Derby 1967–8. 32 t.
17086–17102. Lot No. 30786 Derby 1968. 32 t.

Originally numbered 14056–102. 17090 was numbered 35503 for a time when declassified.

17056		**CH**	RV	*SS*	CP	17090	v	**RR**	H		TM
17058		**N**	H		KT	17091	v	**RR**	H		LT
17064	v	**RR**	H		LT	17096		**G**	MN	*OS*	SL
17077		**RB**	RV	*SS*	CP	17099	v	**RR**	H		LT
17086		**RB**	RV	*SS*	CP	17102		**M**	WC	*SS*	CS

AT5B COUCHETTE/GENERATOR COACH

Dia. AT527. Mark 2B. Formerly part of Royal Train. Converted from a BFK built 1969. Consists of luggage accommodation, guard's compartment, 350 kW diesel generator and staff sleeping accommodation. Pressure ventilated. B5 bogies. ETH 5X.

Lot No. 30888 Wolverton 1977. 46 t.

17105 (14105, 2905)	**0**	RV	*SS*	CP

AB1D (BFK) CORRIDOR BRAKE FIRST

Dia. AB106. Mark 2D. Air conditioned (Stones equipment). 24/– 1T. B4 Bogies. ETH 5.

Lot No. 30823 Derby 1971–72. 33.5 t.

Non-Standard Livery: 17141 & 17164 are as **WV** without lining.

Originally numbered 14141–72.

17141	**0**	RS		FP
17144		RK	*SO*	DY
17146		RK	*SO*	DY
17148		CW		MM
17151		VS		CP
17153	**WR**	RS		CS
17156		RS		DY
17159	**CH**	RV	*SS*	CP
17161		E		OM
17163		VS		CO
17164	**0**	RV	*SS*	CP
17165		RS		FP
17166		H		PY
17167	**VN**	VS	*SS*	CP
17168	**M**	WC	*SS*	CS
17169		RS		CS
17170		RS		DY
17171		E		CL
17172		RS		FP

AE1G (BFO) OPEN BRAKE FIRST

Dia. AE101. Mark 3B. Air conditioned. Fitted with hydraulic handbrake. Refurbished with table lamps and burgundy seat trim. 36/– 1T (w 35/– 1T) BT10 bogies. pg. d. ETH 5X.

Lot No. 30990 Derby 1986. 35.81 t.

17173	**V**	P	*VW*	PC
17174	**V**	P	*VW*	PC
17175 w	**V**	P	*VW*	PC

AA21 (SK) CORRIDOR STANDARD

Dia. AA201 (AA202*). Mark 1. There are two variants depending upon whether the standard class compartments have armrests. Each vehicle has eight compartments. All remaining vehicles have metal window frames and melamine interior panelling. Commonwealth bogies. –/48 2T (–/64 2T *). ETH 4.

18729–18893. Lot No. 30685 Derby 1961–62. 36 t.
18955. Lot No. 30686 Derby 1962. 36 t.
19013. Lot No. 30719 Derby 1962. 37 t.

Non-Standard Livery: 19013 is Pilkington's K (green with white/red chevron and light blue block).

f Facelifted with fluorescent lighting.

Originally numbered 25729–26013.

18729 x*f	**CH**	WC	*SS*	CS
18756 x	**M**	WC	*SS*	CS

18767	x	**CH**	WC	*SS* CS
18806	xt	**M**	WC	*SS* CS
18808	x	**M**	WC	*SS* CS
18862	x	**M**	WC	*SS* CS
18893	x	**CH**	WC	*SS* TM
18955	x*f	**M**	WC	*SS* CS
19013	x	**0**	WC	*SS* CS

AB31 (BCK) CORRIDOR BRAKE COMPOSITE

Dia. AB301 (AB302*). Mark 1. There are two variants depending upon whether the standard class compartments have armrests. Each vehicle has two first class and three standard class compartments. 12/18 2T (12/24 2T *). ETH 2.

21224. Lot No. 30245. Metro-Cammell 1958. B4 bogies. 33 t.
21236–21246. Lot No. 30669 Swindon 1961–62. Commonwealth bogies. 36 t.
21252–21256. Lot No. 30731 Derby 1963. Commonwealth bogies. 37 t.
21266–21272. Lot No. 30732 Derby 1964. Commonwealth bogies. 37 t.

Non-standard Livery: 21269 is British racing green & cream.

21224		**VN**	VS	*SS*	CP
21236	v	**M**	ER		ZG
21241	x	**M**	BK	*SS*	BT
21245	x	**CC**	RS	*SS*	BN
21246		**BG**	RS	*SS*	BN
21252	v	**G**	MH	*SS*	RL
21256	x	**M**	WC	*SS*	CS
21266	*	**M**	WC	*SS*	CS
21268	*		FS		SZ
21269	*	**0**	RS	*SS*	BN
21272	x*	**CH**	RV	*SS*	CP

AB21 (BSK) CORRIDOR BRAKE STANDARD

Dia. AB201 (AB202*). Mark 1. There are two variants depending upon whether the standard class compartments have armrests. Each vehicle has four compartments. Lots 30699 and 30721 have metal window frames and melamine interior panelling. –/24 1T (–/32 1T*). ETH2.

g Fitted with an e.t.s. generator.

34525. Lot No. 30095 Wolverton 1955. Commonwealth bogies. 36 t.
34991. Lot No. 30229 Metro-Cammell 1956–57. Commonwealth bogies. 36 t.
35185–35207. Lot No. 30427 Wolverton 1959. B4 bogies. 33 t.
35317–35333. Lot No. 30699 Wolverton 1962–63. Commonwealth bogies. 37 t.
35407, 35452–35486. Lot No. 30721 Wolverton 1963. Commonwealth Bogies. 37 t.

Non-Standard Livery: 35322 and 35407 are in London & North Western Railway livery.

34525	g	**M**	GS		CS
34991	*	**PC**	VS	*SS*	SL
35185	x	**M**	BK	*SS*	BT
35207	x*	**CC**	VS		SL
35317	x	**G**	WT	*OS*	BQ
35322	x	**0**	SH	*SS*	CJ
35329	v	**G**	MH	*SS*	RL
35333	x	**CH**	24	*OS*	DI
35407	xg	**0**	SH	*SS*	CJ
35452	x	**RR**	H		CP
35453	x	**CH**	RV	*SS*	CP
35457	v	**M**	IE	*OS*	NY
35459	x	**M**	WC	*SS*	CS
35461	x	**CH**	RV	*OS*	CP
35463	v	**M**	WC	*OS*	CS
35465	x	**WV**	LW	*OS*	CP
35468	v	**M**	NR	*OS*	YK
35469	xg	**M**	RS	*SS*	BN
35470	v	**CH**	VT	*OS*	TM
35476	v	**CC**	62	*OS*	SK
35479	v	**M**	SV	*OS*	KR
35486	v	**M**	SV	*OS*	KR

AB1C (BSK) CORRIDOR BRAKE FIRST

Dia. AB103. Mark 2C. Pressure ventilated. Renumbered when declassified. –/24 1T. B4 (g B5) bogies. ETH 4.

Lot No. 30796 Derby 1969–70. 32.5 t.

g Fitted with an e.t.s. generator.

Non-standard Livery: 35511 is British racing green & cream.

35508	(14128, 17128)		**RR**	RV	CP
35511	(14130, 17130)	g	**0**	RA	CP

AB1A (BSK) CORRIDOR BRAKE FIRST

Dia. AB105. Mark 2A. Pressure ventilated. Renumbered when declassified. –/24 1T. B4 bogies. ETH 4.

35510/12–14. Lot No. 30775 Derby 1967–68. 32 t.
35515–18. Lot No. 30786 Derby 1968. 32 t.

* Cage removed from brake compartment.

35510	(14075, 17075)		**RR**	H	KT
35512	(14057, 17057)	*	**RR**	H	CP
35513	(14063, 17063)	*	**RR**	H	KT
35514	(14069, 17069)	*	**RR**	H	CQ
35515	(14079, 17079)	*	**RR**	H	CP
35516	(14080, 17080)	*	**RR**	H	KT
35517	(14088, 17088)	*	**RR**	H	BQ
35518	(14097, 17097)	*	**RR**	H	KT

NAMED COACHES

Dia. The following miscellaneous coaches carry names:

1659	CAMELOT
3105	JULIA
3125	LOCH SHIEL
3130	PAMELA
3174	GLAMIS
3181	MONARCH
3182	WARWICK
3188	SOVEREIGN
3223	DIAMOND
3228	AMETHYST
3240	SAPPHIRE
3244	EMERALD
3247	CHATSWORTH
3267	BELVOIR
3273	ALNWICK
3275	HARLECH
5132	CLAN MUNRO
5154	CLAN FRASER
5193	CLAN MACLEOD
5212	CAPERKAILZIE
5275	Wendy
5307	Beverley
5350	Dawn
5364	Andrea
5365	Deborah
5373	Felicity
5376	Michaela
5378	Sarah
9385	BALMACARA
9388	BAILECHAUL
9417	Ellen
10569	LEVIATHAN
17007	MERCATOR
17077	Catherine
17086	Georgina

2. HIGH SPEED TRAIN TRAILER CARS

HSTs normally run in formations of 7 or 8 trailer cars with a Class 43 power car at each end. All trailer cars are classified Mark 3 and have BT10 bogies with disc brakes and central door locking. Heating is by a 415 V three-phase supply and vehicles have air conditioning. Max. Speed is 125 m.p.h.

All vehicles underwent a mid-life refurbishment in the 1980s, and a further refurbishment programme was completed in November 2000, each train operating company having a different scheme as follows:

First Great Western. Green seat covers and extra partitions between seat bays.
Great North Eastern Railway. New ceiling lighting panels and brown seat covers. First class vehicles have table lamps and imitation walnut plastic end panels.
Virgin Cross-Country. Green seat covers. Standard class vehicles have four seats in the centre of each carriage replaced with a luggage stack.
Virgin West Coast. Red seat covers in first class and light blue seat covers in standard class.
Midland Mainline. Grey seat covers, redesigned seat squabs, side carpeting and two seats in the centre of each carriage replaced with a luggage stack.

All vehicles except TRFK 40501 and TRFM 40619 have been included in this programme.

Tops Type Codes

TOPS type codes for HST trailer cars are made up as follows:

(1) Two letters denoting the layout of the vehicle as follows:

GH Open
GJ Open with Guard's compartment.
GK Buffet
GL Kitchen
GN Buffet

(2) A digit for the class of passenger accommodation

1 First
2 Standard (formerly second)
4 Unclassified

(3) A suffix relating to the build of coach.

G Mark 3

Operator Codes

The normal operator codes are given in brackets after the TOPS codes. These are as follows:

TF	Trailer First	TRFK	Trailer Kitchen First
TGS	Trailer Guard's Standard	TRFM	Trailer Modular Buffet First
TRB	Trailer Buffet First	TRSB	Trailer Buffet Standard
TRFB	Trailer Buffet First	TS	Trailer Standard

GN4G (TRB) TRAILER BUFFET FIRST

Dia. GN401. Converted from TRSB by fitting first class seats. Renumbered from 404xx series by subtracting 200. 23/–. p. q.

40204–40228. Lot No. 30883 Derby 1976–77. 36.12 t.
40231. Lot No. 30899 Derby 1978–79. 36.12 t.

40204	**FG**	A	*GW*	PM
40205	**FG**	A	*GW*	PM
40206	**FG**	A	*GW*	PM
40207	**FG**	A	*GW*	PM
40208	**FG**	A	*GW*	PM
40209	**FG**	A	*GW*	PM
40210	**FG**	A	*GW*	PM
40213	**FG**	A		ZC
40221	**FG**	A	*GW*	PM
40228	**FG**	A	*GW*	PM
40231	**FG**	A	*GW*	PM

GK2G (TRSB) TRAILER BUFFET STANDARD

Dia. GK202. Renumbered from 400xx series by adding 400. –/33 1W. p. q.

40401–40427. Lot No. 30883 Derby 1976–77. 36.12 t.
40429–40437. Lot No. 30899 Derby 1978–79. 36.12 t.

40411/2/32–4 were numbered 40211/2/32–4 for a time when fitted with first class seats.

40401	**V**	P	*VX*	LA
40402	**V**	P	*VX*	LA
40403	**V**	P	*VX*	LA
40411	**V**	P	*VX*	LA
40412	**V**	P	*VX*	LA
40414	**V**	P	*VX*	LA
40415	**V**	P	*VX*	LA
40416	**V**	P	*VX*	LA
40417	**V**	P	*VX*	LA
40418	**V**	P	*VX*	LA
40419	**V**	P	*VX*	LA
40420	**V**	P	*VX*	LA
40422	**V**	P	*VX*	LA
40423	**V**	P	*VX*	LA
40424	**V**	P	*VX*	LA
40425	**V**	P	*VX*	LA
40426	**V**	P	*VX*	LA
40427	**V**	P	*VX*	LA
40429	**V**	P	*VX*	LA
40430	**V**	P	*VX*	LA
40432	**V**	P	*VX*	LA
40433	**V**	P	*VX*	LA
40434	**V**	P	*VX*	LA
40435	**V**	P	*VX*	LA
40436	**V**	P	*VX*	LA
40437	**V**	P	*VX*	LA

GL1G (TRFK) TRAILER KITCHEN FIRST

Dia. GL101. Reclassified from TRUK. p. q. 24/–.

Lot No. 30884 Derby 1976–77. 37 t.

40501		P		ZD

GK1G (TRFM) TRAILER MODULAR BUFFET FIRST

Dia. GK102. Converted to modular catering from TRFB 40719. 17/– 1T. p. q.

Lot No. 30921 Derby 1978–79. 38.16 t.

40619		P	*VX*	LA

GK1G (TRFB) TRAILER BUFFET FIRST

Dia. GK101. These vehicles have larger kitchens than the 402xx and 404xx series vehicles, and are used in trains where full meal service is required. They were renumbered from the 403xx series (in which the seats were unclassified) by adding 400 to previous number. 17/– (*12/– + one seat for staff use). p. q.

40700–40721. Lot No. 30921 Derby 1978–79. 38.16 t.
40722–40735. Lot No. 30940 Derby 1979–80. 38.16 t.
40736–40753. Lot No. 30948 Derby 1980–81. 38.16 t.
40754–40757. Lot No. 30966 Derby 1982. 38.16 t.

40700		**MM**	P	*MM*	NL
40701		**MM**	P	*MM*	NL
40702		**MM**	P	*MM*	NL
40703		**FG**	A	*GW*	LA
40704		**GN**	A	*GN*	EC
40705		**GN**	A	*GN*	EC
40706		**GN**	A	*GN*	EC
40707		**FG**	A	*GW*	LA
40708		**MM**	P	*MM*	NL
40709		**FG**	A	*GW*	LA
40710		**FG**	A	*GW*	LA
40711		**GN**	A	*GN*	EC
40712		**FG**	A	*GW*	LA
40713		**FG**	A	*GW*	LA
40714		**FG**	A	*GW*	PM
40715		**FG**	A	*GW*	PM
40716		**FG**	A	*GW*	PM
40717		**FG**	A	*GW*	PM
40718		**FG**	A	*GW*	LA
40720		**GN**	A	*GN*	EC
40721		**FG**	A	*GW*	LA
40722		**FG**	A	*GW*	LA
40723	*	**V**	A	*VW*	LA
40724		**FG**	A	*GW*	PM
40725		**FG**	A	*GW*	LA
40726		**FG**	A	*GW*	LA
40727		**FG**	A	*GW*	LA
40728		**MM**	P	*MM*	NL
40729		**MM**	P	*MM*	NL
40730		**MM**	P	*MM*	NL
40731		**FG**	A	*GW*	LA
40732		**V**	A	*VW*	LA
40733		**FG**	A	*GW*	LA
40734		**FG**	A	*GW*	PM
40735		**GN**	A	*GN*	EC
40736		**FG**	A	*GW*	LA
40737		**GN**	A	*GN*	EC
40738		**FG**	A	*GW*	LA
40739		**FG**	A	*GW*	PM
40740		**GN**	A	*GN*	EC
40741		**MM**	P	*MM*	NL
40742		**V**	A	*VW*	LA
40743		**FG**	A	*GW*	LA
40744		**FG**	A	*GW*	PM
40745		**FG**	A	*GW*	LA
40746		**MM**	P	*MM*	NL
40747		**FG**	A	*GW*	PM
40748		**GN**	A	*GN*	EC
40749		**MM**	P	*MM*	NL
40750		**GN**	A	*GN*	EC
40751		**MM**	P	*MM*	NL
40752		**FG**	A	*GW*	LA
40753		**MM**	P	*MM*	NL
40754		**MM**	P	*MM*	NL
40755		**FG**	A	*GW*	LA
40756		**MM**	P	*MM*	NL
40757		**FG**	A	*GW*	LA

GH1G (TF) TRAILER FIRST

Dia. GH102. 48/– 2T (w 47/– 2T 1W).

41003–41056. Lot No. 30881 Derby 1976–77. 33.66 t.
41057–41120. Lot No. 30896 Derby 1977–78. 33.66 t.
41121–41148. Lot No. 30938 Derby 1979–80. 33.66 t.
41149–41166. Lot No. 30947 Derby 1980. 33.66 t.

41167–41169. Lot No. 30963 Derby 1982. 33.66 t.
41170. Lot No. 30967 Derby 1982. Former prototype vehicle. 33.66 t.
41179/80. Lot No. 30884 Derby 1976–77. 33.60 t.

s Fitted with centre luggage stack. 46/– 2T 1TD 1W.
41170 was converted from 41001. 41179/80 have been converted from 40505 and 40511 respectively.

41003	p	**FG**	A	*GW*	LA
41004		**FG**	A	*GW*	PM
41005	p	**FW**	A	*GW*	PM
41006		**FG**	A	*GW*	PM
41007	p	**FG**	A	*GW*	PM
41008		**FG**	A	*GW*	PM
41009	p	**FG**	A	*GW*	PM
41010		**FG**	A	*GW*	PM
41011	p	**FG**	A	*GW*	PM
41012		**FG**	A	*GW*	PM
41013	p	**FG**	A	*GW*	PM
41014		**FG**	A	*GW*	PM
41015	p	**FG**	A	*GW*	PM
41016		**FG**	A	*GW*	PM
41017	p	**FG**	A	*GW*	PM
41018		**FG**	A	*GW*	PM
41019	p	**FG**	A	*GW*	PM
41020		**FG**	A	*GW*	PM
41021	p	**FG**	A	*GW*	PM
41022		**FG**	A	*GW*	PM
41023	p	**FG**	A	*GW*	LA
41024		**FG**	A	*GW*	LA
41025	p	**V**	A	*VW*	LA
41026		**V**	A	*VW*	LA
41027	p	**FG**	A	*GW*	LA
41028		**FG**	A	*GW*	LA
41029	p	**FG**	A	*GW*	LA
41030		**FG**	A	*GW*	LA
41031	p	**FG**	A	*GW*	LA
41032		**FG**	A	*GW*	LA
41033	p	**FG**	A	*GW*	LA
41034		**FG**	A	*GW*	LA
41035	p	**V**	A	*VW*	LA
41036	w	**V**	A	*VW*	LA
41037	p	**FG**	A	*GW*	LA
41038		**FG**	A	*GW*	LA
41039		**GN**	A	*GN*	EC
41040		**GN**	A	*GN*	EC
41041	ps	**MM**	P	*MM*	NL
41042		**FG**	A		ZC
41043	w	**GN**	A	*GN*	EC
41044		**GN**	A	*GN*	EC
41045	w	**V**	P	*VX*	LA
41046	s	**MM**	P	*MM*	NL
41051		**FG**	A	*GW*	LA
41052		**FG**	A	*GW*	LA
41055		**FG**	A	*GW*	LA
41056		**FG**	A	*GW*	LA
41057		**MM**	P	*MM*	NL
41058	s	**MM**	P	*MM*	NL
41059	w	**V**	P	*VX*	LA
41060		**FG**	A		ZC
41061		**MM**	P	*MM*	NL
41062	w	**MM**	P	*MM*	NL
41063		**MM**	P	*MM*	NL
41064	s	**MM**	P	*MM*	NL
41065		**FG**	A	*GW*	LA
41066	p	**V**	A	*VW*	LA
41067	s	**MM**	P	*MM*	NL
41068	s	**MM**	P	*MM*	NL
41069	s	**MM**	P	*MM*	NL
41070	s	**MM**	P	*MM*	NL
41071		**MM**	P	*MM*	NL
41072	s	**MM**	P	*MM*	NL
41075		**MM**	P	*MM*	NL
41076	s	**MM**	P	*MM*	NL
41077		**MM**	P	*MM*	NL
41078		**MM**	P	*MM*	NL
41079		**MM**	P	*MM*	NL
41080	s	**MM**	P	*MM*	NL
41081	w	**V**	P	*VX*	LA
41083		**MM**	P	*MM*	NL
41084	s	**MM**	P	*MM*	NL
41085	w	**V**	P	*VX*	LA
41086	w	**V**	P	*VX*	LA
41087		**GN**	A	*GN*	EC
41088	w	**GN**	A	*GN*	EC
41089		**FG**	A	*GW*	LA
41090	w	**GN**	A	*GN*	EC
41091		**GN**	A	*GN*	EC
41092	w	**GN**	A	*GN*	EC
41093		**FG**	A	*GW*	LA
41094		**FG**	A	*GW*	LA
41095	w	**V**	P	*VX*	LA
41096	w	**V**	P	*VX*	LA
41097	w	**GN**	A	*GN*	EC
41098	w	**GN**	A	*GN*	EC
41099		**GN**	A	*GN*	EC

41100	w	**GN**	A	*GN*	EC
41101		**FG**	A	*GW*	LA
41102		**FG**	A	*GW*	LA
41103		**FG**	A	*GW*	LA
41104		**FG**	A	*GW*	LA
41105		**FG**	A	*GW*	PM
41106		**FG**	A	*GW*	PM
41107	w	**V**	P	*VX*	LA
41108	w	**V**	P	*VX*	LA
41109	w	**V**	P	*VX*	LA
41110		**FG**	A	*GW*	PM
41111		**MM**	P	*MM*	NL
41112		**MM**	P	*MM*	NL
41113	s	**MM**	P	*MM*	NL
41114	w	**V**	P	*VX*	LA
41115	w	**V**	P	*VX*	LA
41116		**FG**	A	*GW*	LA
41117		**MM**	P	*MM*	NL
41118	w	**GN**	A	*GN*	EC
41119	w	**V**	P	*VX*	LA
41120		**GN**	A	*GN*	EC
41121	p	**FG**	A	*GW*	LA
41122		**FG**	A	*GW*	LA
41123	p	**FG**	A	*GW*	PM
41124		**FG**	A	*GW*	PM
41125		**FG**	A	*GW*	PM
41126	p	**FG**	A	*GW*	PM
41127	p	**FG**	A	*GW*	PM
41128		**FG**	A	*GW*	PM
41129	p	**FG**	A	*GW*	PM
41130		**FG**	A	*GW*	PM
41131	p	**FG**	A	*GW*	LA
41132		**FG**	A	*GW*	LA
41133	p	**FG**	A	*GW*	LA
41134		**FG**	A	*GW*	LA
41135	p	**FG**	A	*GW*	LA
41136		**FG**	A	*GW*	LA
41137	p	**FG**	A	*GW*	PM
41138		**FG**	A	*GW*	PM
41139	p	**FG**	A	*GW*	LA
41140		**FG**	A	*GW*	LA
41141	p	**FG**	A	*GW*	PM
41142		**FG**	A	*GW*	PM
41143	p	**FG**	A	*GW*	LA
41144		**FG**	A	*GW*	LA
41145	p	**FG**	A	*GW*	PM
41146		**FG**	A	*GW*	PM
41147	w	**V**	P	*VX*	LA
41148	w	**V**	P	*VX*	LA
41149	w	**V**	P	*VX*	LA
41150	w	**GN**	A	*GN*	EC
41151		**GN**	A	*GN*	EC
41152		**GN**	A	*GN*	EC
41153		**MM**	P	*MM*	NL
41154	s	**MM**	P	*MM*	NL
41155		**MM**	P	*MM*	NL
41156		**MM**	P	*MM*	NL
41157		**FG**	A	*GW*	LA
41158		**FG**	A	*GW*	LA
41159	w	**V**	P	*VX*	LA
41160	w	**V**	P	*VX*	LA
41161	w	**V**	P	*VX*	LA
41162	w	**V**	P	*VX*	LA
41163	w	**V**	P	*VX*	LA
41164	p	**V**	A	*VW*	LA
41165	w	**V**	P	*VX*	LA
41166	w	**V**	P	*VX*	LA
41167	w	**V**	P	*VX*	LA
41168	w	**V**	P	*VX*	LA
41169	w	**V**	P	*VX*	LA
41170		**GN**	A	*GN*	EC
41179		**FG**	A	*GW*	PM
41180		**FG**	A	*GW*	PM

GH2G (TS) TRAILER STANDARD

Dia. GH203. –/76 2T. (§ –/70 2T 2W).

42003–42090/42362. Lot No. 30882 Derby 1976–77. 33.60 t.
42091–42250. Lot No. 30897 Derby 1977–79. 33.60 t.
42251–42305. Lot No. 30939 Derby 1979–80. 33.60 t.
42306–42322. Lot No. 30969 Derby 1982. 33.60 t.
42323–42341. Lot No. 30983 Derby 1984–85. 33.60 t.
42342/60. Lot No. 30949 Derby 1982. 33.47 t. Converted from TGS.
42343/5. Lot No. 30970 Derby 1982. 33.47 t. Converted from TGS.
42344/61. Lot No. 30964 Derby 1982. 33.47 t. Converted from TGS.
42346/7/50/1. Lot No. 30881 Derby 1976–77. 33.66 t. Converted from TF.

42348/9/63. Lot No. 30896 Derby 1977–78. 33.66 t. Converted from TF.
42353/5–7. Lot No. 30967 Derby 1982. Ex prototype vehicles. 33.66 t.
42352/4. Lot No. 30897 Derby 1977. Were TF from 1983 to 1992. 33.66 t.

s Centre luggage stack –/72 2T.
t Centre luggage stack –/72 2T. Fitted with pt.
u Centre luggage stack –/74 2T (w –72 2T 1W).
* disabled persons toilet and 5 tip-up seats. –/65 1T 1TD.
42158 was also numbered 41177 for a time when fitted with first class seats.

42003		**FG**	A	*GW*	PM
42004	*	**FG**	A	*GW*	LA
42005		**FG**	A	*GW*	PM
42006		**FG**	A	*GW*	PM
42007	*	**FG**	A	*GW*	LA
42008	*	**FG**	A	*GW*	PM
42009		**FG**	A	*GW*	PM
42010		**FG**	A	*GW*	PM
42012	*	**FG**	A	*GW*	PM
42013		**FG**	A	*GW*	PM
42014		**FG**	A	*GW*	PM
42015	*	**FG**	A	*GW*	PM
42016		**FG**	A	*GW*	PM
42017		**FG**	A	*GW*	PM
42018	*	**FG**	A	*GW*	PM
42019		**FG**	A	*GW*	PM
42020		**FG**	A	*GW*	PM
42021	*	**FG**	A	*GW*	PM
42022		**FG**	A	*GW*	PM
42023		**FG**	A	*GW*	PM
42024	*	**FG**	A	*GW*	PM
42025		**FG**	A	*GW*	PM
42026		**FG**	A	*GW*	PM
42027		**FG**	A	*GW*	PM
42028		**FG**	A	*GW*	PM
42029		**FG**	A	*GW*	PM
42030	*	**FG**	A	*GW*	PM
42031		**FG**	A	*GW*	PM
42032		**FG**	A	*GW*	PM
42033		**FG**	A	*GW*	LA
42034		**FG**	A	*GW*	LA
42035		**FG**	A	*GW*	LA
42036		**V**	A	*VW*	LA
42037		**V**	A	*VW*	LA
42038		**V**	A	*VW*	LA
42039		**FG**	A	*GW*	LA
42040		**FG**	A	*GW*	LA
42041		**FG**	A	*GW*	LA
42042		**FG**	A	*GW*	LA
42043		**FG**	A	*GW*	LA
42044		**FG**	A	*GW*	LA
42045		**FG**	A	*GW*	LA
42046		**FG**	A	*GW*	LA
42047		**FG**	A	*GW*	LA
42048		**FG**	A	*GW*	LA
42049		**FG**	A	*GW*	LA
42050		**FG**	A	*GW*	LA
42051	§	**V**	A	*VW*	LA
42052		**V**	A	*VW*	LA
42053		**V**	A	*VW*	LA
42054		**FG**	A	*GW*	PM
42055		**FG**	A	*GW*	LA
42056		**FG**	A	*GW*	LA
42057		**GN**	A	*GN*	EC
42058		**GN**	A	*GN*	EC
42059		**GN**	A	*GN*	EC
42060		**FG**	A	*GW*	PM
42061		**FG**	A	*GW*	PM
42062	*	**FG**	A	*GW*	LA
42063		**GN**	A	*GN*	EC
42064		**GN**	A	*GN*	EC
42065		**GN**	A	*GN*	EC
42066	*	**FG**	A	*GW*	LA
42067		**FG**	A	*GW*	LA
42068		**FG**	A	*GW*	LA
42069	*	**FG**	A	*GW*	PM
42070		**FG**	A	*GW*	PM
42071		**FG**	A	*GW*	PM
42072		**FG**	A	*GW*	PM
42073		**FG**	A	*GW*	PM
42074		**FG**	A	*GW*	PM
42075		**FG**	A	*GW*	PM
42076		**FG**	A	*GW*	LA
42077		**FG**	A	*GW*	LA
42078		**FG**	A	*GW*	LA
42079		**FG**	A	*GW*	PM
42080		**FG**	A	*GW*	PM
42081	*	**FG**	A	*GW*	LA
42082	*	**FG**	A		ZC
42083		**FG**	A	*GW*	LA
42084	s	**V**	P	*VX*	LA
42085	t	**V**	P	*VX*	LA
42086	s	**V**	P	*VX*	LA
42087	s	**V**	P	*VX*	LA

42088	s	**V**	P	*VX*	LA
42089		**FG**	A	*GW*	PM
42090	s	**V**	P	*VX*	LA
42091	s	**V**	P	*VX*	LA
42092	s	**V**	P	*VX*	LA
42093	s	**V**	P	*VX*	LA
42094	s	**V**	P	*VX*	LA
42095	s	**V**	P	*VX*	LA
42096		**FG**	A	*GW*	LA
42097	§	**V**	A	*VW*	LA
42098		**FG**	A	*GW*	PM
42099		**FG**	A	*GW*	LA
42100	u	**MM**	P	*MM*	NL
42101	uw	**MM**	P	*MM*	NL
42102	u	**MM**	P	*MM*	NL
42103	s	**V**	P	*VX*	LA
42104		**GN**	A	*GN*	EC
42105	s	**V**	P	*VX*	LA
42106		**GN**	A	*GN*	EC
42107		**FG**	A	*GW*	LA
42108	s	**V**	P	*VX*	LA
42109	s	**V**	P	*VX*	LA
42110	s	**V**	P	*VX*	LA
42111	u	**MM**	P	*MM*	NL
42112	u	**MM**	P	*MM*	NL
42113	u	**MM**	P	*MM*	NL
42115	t	**V**	P	*VX*	LA
42116	s	**V**	P	*VX*	LA
42117	s	**V**	P	*VX*	LA
42118		**FG**	A	*GW*	PM
42119	u	**MM**	P	*MM*	NL
42120	u	**MM**	P	*MM*	NL
42121	u	**MM**	P	*MM*	NL
42122		**V**	A	*VW*	LA
42123	u	**MM**	P	*MM*	NL
42124	u	**MM**	P	*MM*	NL
42125	u	**MM**	P	*MM*	NL
42126		**FG**	A	*GW*	LA
42127	s	**V**	P	*VX*	LA
42128	s	**V**	P	*VX*	LA
42129		**FG**	A	*GW*	LA
42130	t	**V**	P	*VX*	LA
42131	u	**MM**	P	*MM*	NL
42132	u	**MM**	P	*MM*	NL
42133	u	**MM**	P	*MM*	NL
42134		**V**	A	*VW*	LA
42135	u	**MM**	P	*MM*	NL
42136	u	**MM**	P	*MM*	NL
42137	u	**MM**	P	*MM*	NL
42138	*	**FG**	A	*GW*	PM
42139	u	**MM**	P	*MM*	NL
42140	u	**MM**	P	*MM*	NL
42141	u	**MM**	P	*MM*	NL
42143		**FG**	A	*GW*	LA
42144		**FG**	A	*GW*	LA
42145		**FG**	A	*GW*	LA
42146		**GN**	A	*GN*	EC
42147	u	**MM**	P	*MM*	NL
42148	u	**MM**	P	*MM*	NL
42149	u	**MM**	P	*MM*	NL
42150		**GN**	A	*GN*	EC
42151	uw	**MM**	P	*MM*	NL
42152	u	**MM**	P	*MM*	NL
42153	u	**MM**	P	*MM*	NL
42154		**GN**	A	*GN*	EC
42155	uw	**MM**	P	*MM*	NL
42156	u	**MM**	P	*MM*	NL
42157	u	**MM**	P	*MM*	NL
42158		**GN**	A	*GN*	EC
42159	s	**V**	P	*VX*	LA
42160	s	**V**	P	*VX*	LA
42161	s	**V**	P	*VX*	LA
42162	s	**V**	P	*VX*	LA
42163	uw	**MM**	P	*MM*	NL
42164	u	**MM**	P	*MM*	NL
42165	u	**MM**	P	*MM*	NL
42166	t	**V**	P	*VX*	LA
42167	s	**V**	P	*VX*	LA
42168	t	**V**	P	*VX*	LA
42169	s	**V**	P	*VX*	LA
42170	s	**V**	P	*VX*	LA
42171		**GN**	A	*GN*	EC
42172		**GN**	A	*GN*	EC
42173	s	**V**	P	*VX*	LA
42174	s	**V**	P	*VX*	LA
42175	s	**V**	P	*VX*	LA
42176	t	**V**	P	*VX*	LA
42177	s	**V**	P	*VX*	LA
42178	t	**V**	P	*VX*	LA
42179		**GN**	A	*GN*	EC
42180		**GN**	A	*GN*	EC
42181		**GN**	A	*GN*	EC
42182		**GN**	A	*GN*	EC
42183	*	**FG**	A	*GW*	LA
42184		**FG**	A	*GW*	LA
42185		**FG**	A	*GW*	LA
42186		**GN**	A	*GN*	EC
42187	t	**V**	P	*VX*	LA
42188	s	**V**	P	*VX*	LA
42189	s	**V**	P	*VX*	LA
42190		**GN**	A	*GN*	EC
42191		**GN**	A	*GN*	EC

42192		**GN**	A	*GN*	EC
42193		**GN**	A	*GN*	EC
42194	uw	**MM**	P	*MM*	NL
42195	s	**V**	P	*VX*	LA
42196		**FG**	A	*GW*	LA
42197		**FG**	A	*GW*	PM
42198		**GN**	A	*GN*	EC
42199		**GN**	A	*GN*	EC
42200	*	**FG**	A	*GW*	LA
42201	*	**FG**	A	*GW*	LA
42202	*	**FG**	A	*GW*	LA
42203		**FG**	A	*GW*	LA
42204		**FG**	A	*GW*	LA
42205	u	**MM**	P	*MM*	NL
42206	*	**FG**	A	*GW*	LA
42207	*	**FG**	A	*GW*	LA
42208		**FG**	A	*GW*	LA
42209		**FG**	A	*GW*	LA
42210	u	**MM**	P	*MM*	NL
42211	*	**FG**	A	*GW*	PM
42212		**FG**	A	*GW*	PM
42213		**FG**	A	*GW*	PM
42214		**FG**	A	*GW*	PM
42215		**GN**	A	*GN*	EC
42216		**FG**	A	*GW*	LA
42217	t	**V**	P	*VX*	LA
42218	t	**V**	P	*VX*	LA
42219		**GN**	A	*GN*	EC
42220	uw	**MM**	P	*MM*	NL
42221		**FG**	A	*GW*	LA
42222	t	**V**	P	*VX*	LA
42223	s	**V**	P	*VX*	LA
42224	s	**V**	P	*VX*	LA
42225	u	**MM**	P	*MM*	NL
42226		**GN**	A	*GN*	EC
42227	u	**MM**	P	*MM*	NL
42228	u	**MM**	P	*MM*	NL
42229	u	**MM**	P	*MM*	NL
42230	u	**MM**	P	*MM*	NL
42231	s	**V**	P	*VX*	LA
42232	t	**V**	P	*VX*	LA
42233	s	**V**	P	*VX*	LA
42234	s	**V**	P	*VX*	LA
42235		**GN**	A	*GN*	EC
42236		**FG**	A	*GW*	PM
42237	s	**V**	P	*VX*	LA
42238	s	**V**	P	*VX*	LA
42239	s	**V**	P	*VX*	LA
42240		**GN**	A	*GN*	EC
42241		**GN**	A	*GN*	EC
42242		**GN**	A	*GN*	EC
42243		**GN**	A	*GN*	EC
42244		**GN**	A	*GN*	EC
42245		**FG**	A	*GW*	LA
42246	s	**V**	P	*VX*	LA
42247	t	**V**	P	*VX*	LA
42248	s	**V**	P	*VX*	LA
42249	s	**V**	P	*VX*	LA
42250		**FG**	A	*GW*	LA
42251	*	**FG**	A	*GW*	PM
42252		**FG**	A	*GW*	LA
42253		**FG**	A	*GW*	LA
42254	s	**V**	P	*VX*	LA
42255	*	**FG**	A	*GW*	PM
42256		**FG**	A	*GW*	PM
42257		**FG**	A	*GW*	PM
42258	t	**V**	P	*VX*	LA
42259	*	**FG**	A	*GW*	PM
42260		**FG**	A	*GW*	PM
42261		**FG**	A	*GW*	PM
42262	s	**V**	P	*VX*	LA
42263		**FG**	A	*GW*	PM
42264	*	**FG**	A	*GW*	PM
42265		**FG**	A	*GW*	LA
42266	s	**V**	P	*VX*	LA
42267	*	**FG**	A	*GW*	PM
42268	*	**FG**	A	*GW*	LA
42269		**FG**	A	*GW*	PM
42270	s	**V**	P	*VX*	LA
42271	*	**FG**	A	*GW*	LA
42272		**FG**	A	*GW*	LA
42273		**FG**	A	*GW*	LA
42274	t	**V**	P	*VX*	LA
42275	*	**FG**	A	*GW*	LA
42276		**FG**	A	*GW*	LA
42277		**FG**	A	*GW*	LA
42278	s	**V**	P	*VX*	LA
42279	*	**FG**	A	*GW*	LA
42280		**FG**	A	*GW*	LA
42281		**FG**	A	*GW*	LA
42282	s	**V**	P	*VX*	LA
42283		**FG**	A	*GW*	LA
42284		**FG**	A	*GW*	PM
42285		**FG**	A	*GW*	PM
42286	s	**V**	P	*VX*	LA
42287	*	**FG**	A	*GW*	LA
42288		**FG**	A	*GW*	LA
42289		**FG**	A	*GW*	LA
42290	t	**V**	P	*VX*	LA
42291	*	**FG**	A	*GW*	PM
42292	*	**FG**	A	*GW*	LA
42293		**FG**	A	*GW*	PM

42294	s	**V**	P	*VX*	LA
42295	*	**FG**	A	*GW*	LA
42296		**FG**	A	*GW*	LA
42297		**FG**	A	*GW*	LA
42298	s	**V**	P	*VX*	LA
42299	*	**FG**	A	*GW*	PM
42300		**FG**	A	*GW*	PM
42301		**FG**	A	*GW*	PM
42302	s	**V**	P	*VX*	LA
42303	t	**V**	P	*VX*	LA
42304	s	**V**	P	*VX*	LA
42305	s	**V**	P	*VX*	LA
42306	s	**V**	P	*VX*	LA
42307	s	**V**	P	*VX*	LA
42308	s	**V**	P	*VX*	LA
42309	s	**V**	P	*VX*	LA
42310	s	**V**	P	*VX*	LA
42311	t	**V**	P	*VX*	LA
42312	s	**V**	P	*VX*	LA
42313	s	**V**	P	*VX*	LA
42314	s	**V**	P	*VX*	LA
42315	t	**V**	P	*VX*	LA
42316	s	**V**	P	*VX*	LA
42317	s	**V**	P	*VX*	LA
42318	s	**V**	P	*VX*	LA
42319	t	**V**	P	*VX*	LA
42320	s	**V**	P	*VX*	LA
42321	s	**V**	P	*VX*	LA
42322	s	**V**	P	*VX*	LA
42323		**GN**	A	*GN*	EC
42324	uw	**MM**	P	*MM*	NL
42325		**FG**	A	*GW*	PM
42326	s	**V**	P	*VX*	LA
42327	uw	**MM**	P	*MM*	NL
42328	uw	**MM**	P	*MM*	NL
42329	uw	**MM**	P	*MM*	NL
42330	s	**V**	P	*VX*	LA
42331	uw	**MM**	P	*MM*	NL
42332		**FG**	A	*GW*	PM
42333		**FG**	A	*GW*	LA
42334	s	**V**	P	*VX*	LA
42335	uw	**MM**	P	*MM*	NL
42336	s	**V**	P	*VX*	LA
42337	uw	**MM**	P	*MM*	NL
42338	s	**V**	P	*VX*	LA
42339	uw	**MM**	P	*MM*	NL
42340		**GN**	A	*GN*	EC
42341	uw	**MM**	P	*MM*	NL

42342	(44082)		**V**	A	*VW*	LA
42343	(44095)		**FG**	A	*GW*	LA
42344	(44092)	*	**FG**	A	*GW*	PM
42345	(44096)	*	**FG**	A	*GW*	LA
42346	(41053)		**FG**	A	*GW*	PM
42347	(41054)	*	**FG**	A	*GW*	PM
42348	(41073)	*	**FG**	A	*GW*	LA
42349	(41074)		**FG**	A	*GW*	PM
42350	(41047)		**FG**	A	*GW*	LA
42351	(41048)		**FG**	A	*GW*	PM
42352	(42142, 41176)	u	**MM**	P	*MM*	NL
42353	(42001, 41171)	s	**V**	P	*VX*	LA
42354	(42114, 41175)		**GN**	A	*GN*	EC
42355	(42000, 41172)	§	**V**	A	*VW*	LA
42356	(42002, 41173)		**FG**	A	*GW*	PM
42357	(41002, 41174)		**V**	A	*VW*	LA
42360	(44084, 45084)		**FG**	A	*VW*	PM
42361	(44099)		**FW**	A	*GW*	PM
42362	(42011, 41178)		**FG**	A	*GW*	PM
42363	(41082)	s	**V**	P	*VX*	LA

GJ2G (TGS) TRAILER GUARD'S STANDARD

Dia. GJ205. –/65 1T (w –/63 1T 1W). pg.
44000. Lot No. 30953 Derby 1980. 33.47 t.
44001–44090. Lot No. 30949 Derby 1980–82. 33.47 t.
44091–44094. Lot No. 30964 Derby 1982. 33.47 t.

44097–44101. Lot No. 30970 Derby 1982. 33.47 t.

s t Fitted with centre luggage stack s –/63 1T, t –/61 1T.

44000	t	**V**	P	*VX*	LA
44001	w	**FG**	A	*GW*	LA
44002	w	**FG**	A	*GW*	PM
44003	w	**FG**	A	*GW*	PM
44004	w	**FG**	A	*GW*	PM
44005	w	**FG**	A	*GW*	PM
44006	w	**FG**	A	*GW*	PM
44007	w	**FG**	A	*GW*	PM
44008	w	**FG**	A	*GW*	PM
44009	w	**FG**	A	*GW*	PM
44010	w	**FG**	A	*GW*	PM
44011	w	**FG**	A	*GW*	LA
44012		**V**	A	*VW*	LA
44013	w	**FG**	A	*GW*	LA
44014	w	**FG**	A	*GW*	LA
44015	w	**FG**	A	*GW*	LA
44016	w	**FG**	A	*GW*	LA
44017		**V**	A	*VW*	LA
44018	w	**FG**	A	*GW*	LA
44019	w	**GN**	A	*GN*	EC
44020	w	**FG**	A	*GW*	PM
44021	t	**V**	P	*VX*	LA
44022	w	**FG**	A	*GW*	LA
44023	w	**FW**	A	*GW*	PM
44024	w	**FG**	A	*GW*	PM
44025	w	**FG**	A	*GW*	LA
44026	w	**FG**	A	*GW*	PM
44027	s	**MM**	P	*MM*	NL
44028	w	**FG**	A	*GW*	LA
44029	w	**FG**	A	*GW*	PM
44030	w	**FG**	A	*GW*	PM
44031		**V**	A	*VW*	LA
44032	w	**FG**	A	*GW*	PM
44033	w	**FG**	A	*GW*	LA
44034	w	**FG**	A	*GW*	LA
44035	w	**FG**	A	*GW*	LA
44036	w	**FG**	A	*GW*	PM
44037	w	**FG**	A	*GW*	LA
44038	w	**FG**	A	*GW*	PM
44039	w	**FG**	A	*GW*	LA
44040	w	**FG**	A	*GW*	PM
44041	s	**MM**	P	*MM*	NL
44042	t	**V**	P	*VX*	LA
44043	w	**FG**	A	*GW*	LA
44044	s	**MM**	P	*MM*	NL
44045	w	**GN**	A	*GN*	EC
44046	s	**MM**	P	*MM*	NL
44047	s	**MM**	P	*MM*	NL
44048	s	**MM**	P	*MM*	NL
44049	w	**FG**	A	*GW*	LA
44050	s	**MM**	P	*MM*	NL
44051	s	**MM**	P	*MM*	NL
44052	s	**MM**	P	*MM*	NL
44053	t	**V**	P	*VX*	LA
44054	s	**MM**	P	*MM*	NL
44055	t	**V**	P	*VX*	LA
44056	w	**GN**	A	*GN*	EC
44057	t	**V**	P	*VX*	LA
44058	w	**GN**	A	*GN*	EC
44059	w	**FG**	A	*GW*	LA
44060	t	**V**	P	*VX*	LA
44061	w	**GN**	A	*GN*	EC
44062	t	**V**	P	*VX*	LA
44063	w	**GN**	A	*GN*	EC
44064	w	**FG**	A	*GW*	LA
44065	t	**V**	P	*VX*	LA
44066	w	**FG**	A	*GW*	LA
44067	w	**FG**	A	*GW*	PM
44068	t	**V**	P	*VX*	LA
44069	t	**V**	P	*VX*	LA
44070	s	**MM**	P	*MM*	NL
44071	s	**MM**	P	*MM*	NL
44072	t	**V**	P	*VX*	LA
44073	s	**MM**	P	*MM*	NL
44074	t	**V**	P	*VX*	LA
44075	t	**V**	P	*VX*	LA
44076	t	**V**	P	*VX*	LA
44077	w	**GN**	A	*GN*	EC
44078	t	**V**	P	*VX*	LA
44079	t	**V**	P	*VX*	LA
44080	w	**GN**	A	*GN*	EC
44081	t	**V**	P	*VX*	LA
44083	s	**MM**	P	*MM*	NL
44085	s	**MM**	P	*MM*	NL
44086	w	**FG**	A	*GW*	LA
44087	t	**V**	P	*VX*	LA
44088	t	**V**	P	*VX*	LA
44089	t	**V**	P	*VX*	LA
44090	t	**V**	P	*VX*	LA
44091	t	**V**	P	*VX*	LA
44093	w	**FG**	A	*GW*	LA
44094	w	**GN**	A	*GN*	EC
44097	t	**V**	P	*VX*	LA
44098	w	**GN**	A	*GN*	EC
44100	t	**V**	P	*VX*	LA
44101	t	**V**	P	*VX*	LA

3. SALOONS

Several specialist passenger carrying vehicles, normally referred to as saloons are permitted to run on the Railtrack system. Many of these are to pre-nationalisation designs.

LNER GENERAL MANAGERS SALOON

Dia. AO133. Built 1945 by LNER, York. Gangwayed at one end with a verandah at the other. The interior has a dining saloon seating twelve, kitchen, toilet, office and nine seat lounge. 21/– 1T. B4 bogies. 75 m.p.h. ETH3. 35.7 t.

1999 (902260) **M** GS *SS* ML

GNR FIRST CLASS SALOON

Dia. AO132. Built 1912 by GNR, Doncaster. Contains entrance vestibule, lavatory, two seperate saloons, library and luggage space. Gresley bogies. 19/– 1T. 75 m.p.h. 29.4 t.

Non-Standard Livery: Teak.

4807 (807) x **0** SH *SS* CJ

LNWR DINING SALOON

Dia. AO131. Built 1890 by LNWR, Wolverton. Mounted on the underframe of LMS GUV 37908 in the 1980s. Contains kitchen and dining area seating 12 at tables for two. Gresley bogies. 10/–. 75 m.p.h. 25.4 t.

Non-Standard Livery: London & North Western Railway.

5159 (159) x **0** SH *SS* CJ

GENERAL MANAGER'S SALOON

Dia. AZ501. Renumbered 1989 from London Midland Region departmental series. Formerly the LMR General Manager's saloon. Rebuilt from LMS period 1 BFK M 5033 M to dia. 1654 and mounted on the underframe of BR suburban BS M 43232. Screw couplings have been removed. B4 bogies. 100 m.p.h. ETH2X.

LMS Lot No. 326 Derby 1927. 27.5 t.

Non-Standard Livery: Aircraft blue with gold lining.

6320 (5033, DM 395707) x **0** 62 *SS* SK

GWR FIRST CLASS SALOON

Dia. AO103. Built 1930 by GWR, Swindon. Contains saloons at either end with body end observation windows, staff compartment, central kitchen and pantry/bar. Numbered DE321011 when in departmental service with British Railways. 20/– 1T. GWR bogies. 75 m.p.h. 34 t.

GWR Lot No. 1431 1930.

9004	**CH**	RA	*ON*	CP

WCJS OBSERVATION SALOON

Dia. AO102. Built 1892 by LNWR, Wolverton. Originally dining saloon mounted on six-wheel bogies. Rebuilt with new underframe with four-wheel bogies in 1927. Rebuilt 1960 as observation saloon with DMU end. Gangwayed at other end. The interior has a saloon, kitchen, guards vestibule and observation lounge. Gresley bogies. 19/– 1T. 28.5 t. 75 m.p.h.

Non-Standard Livery: London & North Western Railway.

45018 (484, 15555)	x	**0**	SH	*SS*	CJ

LMS INSPECTION SALOONS

Dia. QX035 (*QX504). Built as engineers inspection saloons. Non-gangwayed. Observation windows at each end. The interior layout consists of two saloons interspersed by a central lavatory/kitchen/guards section. BR Mark 1 bogies. 80 m.p.h. 31.5 t.

45020–45026. Lot No. LMS 1356 Wolverton 1944.
45029. Lot No. LMS 1327 Wolverton 1942.
999503–999504. Lot No. BR Wagon Lot. 3093 Wolverton 1957.

45026 & 999503 are currently hired to Racal-BRT who have contracted maintenance to the Severn Valley Railway.

45020		**E**	E	*SS*	TO
45026	v	**M**	E	*SS*	KR
45029	v	**E**	E	*SS*	ML
999503	v*	**M**	E	*SS*	KR
999504	v*	**E**	E	*SS*	TO

RAILFILMS KITCHEN/SLEEPING SALOON

Dia. AO . Converted from BR Mark 1 SK. Contains three sleeping cabins with showers and toilets and a large kitchen/pantry. Commonwealth bogies. 100 m.p.h. ETH 4.

Non-standard Livery: London & North Western Railway.

99884 (26208, 19208)	**0**	RA	CP	State Car No. 84

ROYAL SCOTSMAN SALOONS

Built 1960 by Metro-Cammell as Pullman Parlour First (§Pullman Kitchen First) for East Coast Main Line services. Rebuilt 1990 as sleeping cars with four twin sleeping rooms (*§ three twin sleeping rooms and two single sleeping rooms at each end). Commonwealth bogies. 38.5 t.

99961 (324 AMBER) *	M	GS	*SS*	ML	STATE CAR 1
99962 (329 PEARL)	M	GS	*SS*	ML	STATE CAR 2
99963 (324 TOPAZ)	M	GS	*SS*	ML	STATE CAR 3
99964 (313 FINCH) §	M	GS	*SS*	ML	STATE CAR 4

Built 1960 by Metro-Cammell as Pullman Kitchen First for East Coast Main Line services. Rebuilt 1990 as observation car with open verandah seating 32. Commonwealth bogies. 38.5 t.

99965 (319 SNIPE)	M	GS	*SS*	ML	OBSERVATION CAR

Built 1960 by Metro-Cammell as Pullman Kitchen First for East Coast Main Line services. Rebuilt 1993 as dining car. Commonwealth bogies. 38.5 t.

99967 (317 RAVEN)	M	GS	*SS*	ML	DINING CAR

Mark 3A. Converted from SLEP at Carnforth Railway Restoration and Engineering Services in 1997. BT10 bogies. Attendant's and adjacent two sleeping compartments converted to generator room containing a 160 kW Volvo unit. In 99968 four sleeping compartments remain for staff use with another converted for use as a staff shower and toilet. The remaining five sleeping compartments have been replaced by two passenger cabins. In 99969 seven sleeping compartments remain for staff use. A further sleeping compartment, along with one toilet, have been converted to store rooms. The other two sleeping compartments have been combined to form a crew mess. ETH7X. 41.5 t.

Lot. No. 30960 Derby 1981–3.

99968 (10541)	M	GS	*SS*	ML	STATE CAR 5
99969 (10556)	M	GS	*SS*	ML	SERVICE CAR

RAILFILMS 'LMS CLUB CAR'

Dia. AO239. Converted from BR Mark 1 TSO at Carnforth Railway Restoration and Engineering Services in 1994. Contains kitchenette, pantry, coupé, lounge/reception area with two setees and two dining saloons. 24/– 1T. Commonwealth bogies. 100 m.p.h. ETH 4.

Lot. No. 30724 York 1963. 37 t.

99993 (5067)	M	RA	*SS*	CP	LMS CLUB CAR

BR INSPECTION SALOON

Dia. QX505. Mark 1. Short frames. Non-gangwayed. Observation windows at each end. The interior layout consists of two saloons interspersed by a central lavatory/kitchen/guards/luggage section. BR Mark 1 bogies. 90 m.p.h.

Lot No. BR Wagon Lot. 3379 Swindon 1960. 30.5 t.

999509	E	E	*SS*	ML

4. PULLMAN CAR COMPANY SERIES

Pullman cars have never generally been numbered as such, although many have carried numbers, instead they have carried titles. However, a scheme of schedule numbers exists which generally lists cars in chronological order. In this section those numbers are shown followed by the cars title. Cars described as 'kitchen' contain a kitchen in addition to passenger accomodation and have gas cooking unless otherwise stated. Cars described as 'parlour' consist entirely of passenger accomodation. Cars described as 'brake' contain a compartment for the use of the guard and a luggage compartment in addition to passenger accommodation.

PULLMAN PARLOUR FIRST

Built 1927 by Midland Carriage and Wagon Company. Gresley bogies. 26/–. ETH 2. 41 t.

213	MINERVA		**PC**	VS	*SS*	SL

PULLMAN BRAKE THIRD

Built 1928 by Metropolitan Carriage and Wagon Company. Gresley bogies. –/30. 37.5 t.

232	CAR No. 79	v	**PC**	NY	*SS*	NY

PULLMAN PARLOUR FIRST

Built 1928 by Metropolitan Carriage and Wagon Company. Gresley bogies. 24/–. ETH 4. 40 t.

239	AGATHA		**PC**	VS		SL
243	LUCILLE		**PC**	VS	*SS*	SL

PULLMAN KITCHEN FIRST

Built 1925 by BRCW. Rebuilt by Midland Carriage & Wagon Company in 1928. Gresley bogies. 20/–. ETH 4. 41 t.

245	IBIS		**PC**	VS	*SS*	SL

PULLMAN PARLOUR FIRST

Built 1928 by Metropolitan Carriage and Wagon Company. Gresley bogies. 24/–. ETH 4.

254	ZENA		**PC**	VS	*SS*	SL

PULLMAN KITCHEN FIRST

Built 1928 by Metropolitan Carriage and Wagon Company. Gresley bogies. 20/–. ETH 4. 42 t.

255	IONE		**PC**	VS	*SS*	SL

PULLMAN PARLOUR THIRD

Built 1931 by Birmingham Railway Carriage and Wagon Company. Gresley bogies. –/42.

261	CAR No. 83		**PC**	VS		SL

PULLMAN KITCHEN COMPOSITE

Built 1932 by Metropolitan Carriage and Wagon Company. Originally included in 6-Pul EMU. Electric cooking. EMU bogies. 12/16.

264	RUTH		**PC**	VS		SL

PULLMAN KITCHEN FIRST

Built 1932 by Metopolitan Carriage and Wagon Company. Originally included in 'Brighton Belle' EMUs but now used as hauled stock. Electric cooking. B5 (SR) bogies (§ EMU bogies). 20/–. ETH 2. 44 t.

280	AUDREY		**PC**	VS	*SS*	SL
281	GWEN		**PC**	VS	*SS*	SL
283	MONA	§	**PC**	VS		SL
284	VERA		**PC**	VS	*SS*	SL

PULLMAN PARLOUR THIRD

Built 1932 by Metropolitan Carriage and Wagon Company. Originally included in 'Brighton Belle' EMUs. EMU bogies. –/56.

285	CAR No. 85		**PC**	VS		SL
286	CAR No. 86		**PC**	VS		SL

PULLMAN BRAKE THIRD

Built 1932 by Metropolitan Carriage and Wagon Company. Originally driving motor cars in 'Brighton Belle' EMUs. Traction and control equipment removed for use as hauled stock. EMU bogies. –/48.

288	CAR No. 88		**PC**	VS		SL
292	CAR No. 92		**PC**	VS		SL
293	CAR No. 93		**PC**	VS		SL

PULLMAN PARLOUR FIRST

Built 1951 by Birmingham Railway Carriage and Wagon Company. Gresley bogies. 32/–. ETH 3. 39 t.

301 PERSEUS **PC** VS *SS* SL

Dia. AO415. Built 1952 by Pullman Car Company, Preston Park using underframe and bogies from 176 RAINBOW, the body of which had been destroyed by fire. Gresley bogies. 26/–. ETH 4. 38 t.

302 PHOENIX **PC** VS *SS* SL

PULLMAN KITCHEN FIRST

Built 1951 by Birmingham Railway Carriage & Wagon Company. Gresley bogies. 22/–.

307 CARINA **PC** VS SL

PULLMAN PARLOUR FIRST

Built 1951 by Birmingham Railway Carriage & Wagon Company. Gresley bogies. 32/–. ETH 3. 39 t.

308 CYGNUS **PC** VS *SS* SL

PULLMAN FIRST BAR

Built 1951 by Birmingham Railway Carriage & Wagon Company. Rebuilt 1999 by Blake Fabrications, Edinburgh with original timber-framed body replaced by a new fabricated steel body. Contains kitchen, bar, dining saloon and coupé. Electric cooking. Gresley bogies. 14/– 1T. ETH 3.

310 PEGASUS **PC** RA *SS* CP

Also carries "THE TRIANON BAR" branding.

PULLMAN KITCHEN FIRST

Built by Metro-Cammell 1960/1 for East Coast Main-line services. Commonwealth bogies. 20/– 2T. ETH4. 41.2 t.

316 was numbered DB 975608 for a time when in departmental service for British Railways.

315	HERON	x	**PC**	FS		On loan to Great Central Railway
316	MAGPIE	x	**PC**	WC		CS
318	ROBIN	x	**PC**	NY	*SS*	NY
321	SWIFT	x	**PC**	FS		CS

PULLMAN PARLOUR FIRST

Built by Metro-Cammell 1960/1 for East Coast Main-line services. Commonwealth bogies. 29/– 2T. 38.5 t.

325	AMETHYST	x	**PC**	FS		SZ
328	OPAL	x	**PC**	NY	*SS*	NY

PULLMAN KITCHEN SECOND

Built by Metro-Cammell 1960/1 for East Coast Main-line services. Commonwealth bogies. –/30 1T. 40 t.

335	CAR No. 335	x	**PC**	VT	TM
337	CAR No. 337	x	**PC**	FS	CS

PULLMAN PARLOUR SECOND

Built by Metro-Cammell 1960/1 for East Coast Main-line services. Commonwealth bogies. –/42 2T. 38.5 t.

347	CAR No. 347	x	**PC**	VT	TM
348	CAR No. 348	x	**PC**	VT	TM
349	CAR No. 349	x	**PC**	VT	On loan to Kent & East Sussex Railway
350	CAR No. 350	x	**PC**	VT	TM
351	CAR No. 351	x	**PC**	VT	TM
352	CAR No. 352	x	**PC**	VT	TM
353	CAR No. 353	x	**PC**	VT	TM

PULLMAN FIRST BAR

Built by Metro-Cammell 1961 for East Coast Main-line services. Commonwealth bogies. 24/– + bar seating 1T. 38.5 t.

354	THE HADRIAN BAR	x	**PC**	VT	TM

5. PASSENGER COACHING STOCK AWAITING DISPOSAL

This list contains the last known locations of coaching stock awaiting disposal. The definition of which vehicles are "awaiting disposal" is somewhat vague, but generally speaking these are vehicles of types not now in normal service or vehicles which have been damaged by fire, vandalism or collision.

1644	CS
1650	CS
1652	CS
1655	CS
1663	CS
1670	CS
1684	CS
1688	CS
4858	CS
4860	CS
4932	CS
4997	CS
5438	DY
5476	Neville Hill Up Sidings
5505	CS
5533	Neville Hill Up Sidings
5574	Neville Hill Up Sidings
5585	Neville Hill Up Sidings
5595	Neville Hill Up Sidings
5645	CS
5709	CS
5712	CS
6335	LA
6339	EC
6343	HT
6345	EC
6347	ZN
6351	ZF
6356	ZB
6357	ZB
6362	LL
6363	LL
6390	ZB
6523	CS
6900	Cambridge Station Yard
6901	Cambridge Station Yard
9458	ZB
9482	NL
13306	CS
13320	CS
13323	CS
17039	CD
18837	CS
21265	CS
34952	SL
35509	ZH

6. 99xxx RANGE NUMBER CONVERSION TABLE

The following table is presented to help readers identify vehicles which may carry numbers in the 99xxx range, the former private owner number series which is no longer in general use.

99xxx	*BR No.*	*99xxx*	*BR No.*	*99xxx*	*BR No.*	*99xxx*	*BR No.*
99035	35322	99325	5727	99546	281	99723	35459
99041	35476	99326	4954	99566	3066	99782	17007
99052	45018	99327	5044	99568	3068	99792	17019
99121	3105	99328	5033	99670	546	99823	4832
99125	3113	99329	4931	99671	548	99826	13229
99127	3117	99371	3128	99672	549	99827	3096
99128	3130	99405	35486	99673	550	99828	13230
99131	1999	99530	301	99674	551	99829	4856
99304	21256	99531	302	99675	552	99830	5028
99311	1882	99532	308	99676	553	99880	5159
99312	35463	99534	245	99677	586	99881	4807
99314	18729	99535	213	99678	504	99886	35407
99315	18955	99536	254	99679	506	99887	2127
99316	13321	99537	280	99680	17102	99953	35468
99317	3766	99538	34991	99710	18767	99966	34525
99318	4912	99539	255	99712	18893	99970	232
99319	14168	99540	3069	99713	19013	99972	318
99321	5299	99541	243	99716	18808	99973	324
99322	5600	99542	889202	99718	18862	99974	328
99323	5704	99543	284	99721	18756	99995	35457
99324	5714	99545	80207	99722	18806		

7. PRESERVED LOCOMOTIVE SUPPORT COACHES TABLE

The following table lists support coaches and the BR numbers of the locomotives which they normally support at present. These coaches can spend considerable periods of time off the Railtrack network when the locomotives they support are not being used on that network.

17007	35028	35317	34067	35463	WC locos	35476	46233
17013	60103*	35333	6024	35465	46035§	35479	SV locos
17019	45407	35457	62005	35468	NR locos	35486	SV locos
17096	35028	35461	5029	35470	BM locos	80217	75014

* Carries former LNER number 4472.

§ Carries original number D 172.

8. NON-PASSENGER-CARRYING COACHING STOCK

The notes shown for locomotive-hauled passenger stock generally apply also to non-passenger-carrying coaching stock (often abbreviated to NPCCS).

TOPS TYPE CODES

TOPS type codes for NPCCS are made up as follows:

(1) Two letters denoting the type of the vehicle:

AX	Nightstar generator van
AY	Eurostar barrier vehicle
NA	Propelling control vehicle.
NB	High security brake van (100 m.p.h.).
NC	Gangwayed brake van modified for newspaper conveyance (100 m.p.h.).
ND	Gangwayed brake van (90 m.p.h.).
NE	Gangwayed brake van (100 m.p.h.).
NF	Gangwayed brake van with guard's safety equipment removed.
NG	Motorail loading wagon.
NH	Gangwayed brake van (110 m.p.h.).
NI	High security brake van (110 m.p.h.).
NJ	General utility van (90 m.p.h.).
NK	High security general utility van (100 m.p.h.).
NL	Newspaper van.
NN	Courier vehicle.
NO	General utility van (100 m.p.h. e.t.h. wired).
NP	General utility van for post office use or Motorail van (110 m.p.h.).
NQ	High security brake van (110 m.p.h.).
NR	BAA container van (100 m.p.h.).
NS	Post office sorting van.
NT	Post office stowage van.
NU	Brake post office stowage van.
NV	Motorail van (side loading).
NX	Motorail van (100 m.p.h.).
NY	Exhibition van.
NZ	Driving brake van (also known as driving van trailer).
QS	EMU translator vehicle.
YR	Ferry van (special Southern Region version of NJ with two pairs of side doors instead of three).

(2) A third letter denoting the brake type:

A	Air braked
V	Vacuum braked
X	Dual braked

OPERATING CODES

The normal operating codes are given in parentheses after the TOPS type codes. These are as follows:

BG	Gangwayed brake van.
BPOT	Brake post office stowage van.
DLV	Driving brake van (also known as driving van trailer – DVT).
GUV	General utility van.
PCV	Propelling control van.
POS	Post office sorting van.
POT	Post office stowage van.

AK51 (RK) KITCHEN CAR

Dia. AK503. Mark 1. Converted 1989 from RBR. Fluorescent lighting. Commonwealth bogies. ETH 2X.

Lot No. 30628 Pressed Steel 1960–61. 39 t.

Note: Kitchen cars have traditionally been numbered in the NPCCS series, but have passenger coach diagram numbers!

80041	(1690)	x	**CC**	RS	*SS*	BN

NN COURIER VEHICLE

Dia. NN504. Mark 1. Converted 1986–7 from BSKs. One compartment retained for courier use. Roller shutter doors. ETH 2.

80207. Lot No. 30721 Wolverton 1963. Commonwealth bogies. 37 t.
80204/11–7/23. Lot No. 30699 Wolverton 1962. Commonwealth bogies. 37 t.
80220. Lot No. 30573 Gloucester 1960. B4 bogies. 33 t.

Non-Standard Livery: 80211 is purple.

80204	(35297)	x	**M**	62		CS
80207	(35466)	x	**PC**	VS	*SS*	SL
80211	(35296)		**0**	RK		DY
80213	(35316)	x	**CH**	RV	*SS*	CP
80217	(35299)	x	**M**	14	*OS*	NY
80220	(35276)	x	**G**	NE		BQ
80223	(35331)	x	**RY**	RS		DY

Name: 80207 is branded 'BAGGAGE CAR No.11'.

NP POST OFFICE GUV

Dia. NP502. Mark 1. Converted 1991–93 from newspaper vans. Short frames (57'). Originally converted from GUV. Fluorescent lighting, toilet and gangways fitted. Load 14 t. B5 bogies. ETH 3X.

Lot No. 30922 Wolverton or Doncaster 1977–78. 31 t.

80253	(86170, 94018)		**RM**	E	OM
80254	(86082, 94012)	x	**RM**	E	OM
80255	(86098, 94019)	x	**RM**	E	OM
80256	(86408, 94013)	x	**RM**	E	OM
80258	(86651, 94002)		**RM**	E	OM
80259	(86845, 94005)	x	**RM**	E	OM

NS (POS) POST OFFICE SORTING VAN

Used in travelling post office (TPO) trains. Mark 1. Various diagrams. Pressure ventilated. Fluorescent lighting. B5 bogies. ETH 4X.

80319–80327. Dia. NS504. Lot No. 30778 York 1968–69. 35 t.
80331–80337. Dia. NS505. Lot No. 30779 York 1968–69. 35 t.
80339–80355. Dia. NS506. Lot No. 30780 York 1968–69. 35 t.
80356–80380. Dia. NS501. Lot No. 30839 York 1972–73. 37 t.

80319	**RM**	E	*E*	EN
80320	**RM**	E	*E*	EN
80321	**RM**	E	*E*	BK
80322	**RM**	E	*E*	EN
80323	**RM**	E	*E*	EN
80324	**RM**	E	*E*	EN
80325	**RM**	E	*E*	EN
80326	**RM**	E	*E*	EN
80327	**RM**	E	*E*	BK
80331	**RM**	E	*E*	EN
80332	**RM**	E	*E*	EN
80333	**RM**	E	*E*	EN
80334	**RM**	E	*E*	BK
80337	**RM**	E	*E*	EN
80339	**RM**	E	*E*	BK
80340	**RM**	E	*E*	BK
80341	**RM**	E	*E*	EN
80342	**RM**	E	*E*	BK
80343	**RM**	E	*E*	BK
80344	**RM**	E	*E*	BK
80345	**RM**	E	*E*	EN
80346	**RM**	E	*E*	EN
80347	**RM**	E	*E*	EN
80348	**RM**	E	*E*	BK
80349	**RM**	E	*E*	EN
80350	**RM**	E	*E*	BK
80351	**RM**	E	*E*	EN
80352	**RM**	E	*E*	BK
80353	**RM**	E	*E*	EN
80354	**RM**	E	*E*	BK
80355	**RM**	E	*E*	EN
80356	**RM**	E	*E*	BK
80357	**RM**	E	*E*	BK
80358	**RM**	E	*E*	EN
80359	**RM**	E	*E*	BK
80360	**RM**	E	*E*	EN
80361	**RM**	E	*E*	EN
80362	**RM**	E	*E*	EN
80363	**RM**	E	*E*	BK
80364	**RM**	E	*E*	BK
80365	**RM**	E	*E*	EN
80366	**RM**	E	*E*	EN
80367	**RM**	E	*E*	EN
80368	**RM**	E	*E*	BK
80369	**RM**	E	*E*	EN
80370	**RM**	E	*E*	BK
80371	**RM**	E	*E*	BK
80372	**RM**	E	*E*	EN
80373	**RM**	E	*E*	EN
80374	**RM**	E	*E*	EN
80375	**RM**	E	*E*	BK
80376	**RM**	E	*E*	BK
80377	**RM**	E	*E*	EN
80378	**RM**	E	*E*	EN
80379	**RM**	E	*E*	EN
80380	**RM**	E	*E*	BK

Names:

80320 The Borders Mail
80327 George James
80337 Brian Quinn
80360 Derek Carter
80367 M.G. Berry
80368 George Economou

80381–80395. Lot No. 30900 Wolverton 1977. Dia NS531. Converted from SK. 38 t.

80381	(25112)	**RM**	E	*E*	EN
80382	(25109)	**RM**	E	*E*	EN
80383	(25033)	**RM**	E	*E*	EN
80384	(25078)	**RM**	E	*E*	EN
80385	(25083)	**RM**	E	*E*	EN
80386	(25099)	**RM**	E	*E*	EN
80387	(25045)	**RM**	E	*E*	EN
80389	(25103)	**RM**	E		ZG
80390	(25047)	**RM**	E	*E*	EN
80392	(25082)	**RM**	E	*E*	EN

80393	(25118)	**RM**	E	*E*	EN
80394	(25156)	**RM**	E	*E*	EN
80395	(25056)	**RM**	E	*E*	EN

Names:

80384	C W Pennell MBE
80385	Paul Rushton
80390	Ernie Gosling

NT (POT) POST OFFICE STOWAGE VAN

Mark 1. Open vans used for stowage of mail bags in conjunction with POS.

Lot No. 30488 Wolverton 1959. Dia. NT502. Originally built with nets for collecting mail bags in motion. Equipment now removed. B5 bogies. ETH 3. 35 t.

80400	**RM**	E	*E*	BK
80401	**RM**	E	*E*	EN
80402	**RM**	E	*E*	BK

The following eight vehicles were converted at York from BSK to lot 30143 (80403) and 30229 (80404–80414). No new lot number was issued. Dia. NT503. B5 bogies. 35 t. (* Dia. NT501 BR2 bogies 38 t.). ETH 3 (3X*).

80403	(34361)		**RM**	E	*E*	BK
80404	(35014)		**RM**	E	*E*	BK
80405	(35009)		**RM**	E	*E*	BK
80406	(35022)		**RM**	E	*E*	EN
80411	(35003)	*	**RM**	E	*E*	EN
80412	(35002)	*	**RM**	E	*E*	EN
80413	(35004)	*	**RM**	E	*E*	EN
80414	(35005)	*	**RM**	E	*E*	EN

Lot No. 30781 York 1968. Dia. NT505. Pressure ventilated. B5 bogies. ETH 4. 34 t.

80415	**RM**	E	*E*	EN
80416	**RM**	E	*E*	EN
80417	**RM**	E	*E*	EN
80419	**RM**	E	*E*	EN
80420	**RM**	E	*E*	BK
80421	**RM**	E	*E*	EN
80422	**RM**	E	*E*	EN
80423	**RM**	E	*E*	EN
80424	**RM**	E	*E*	EN

Lot No. 30840 York 1973. Dia. NT504. Pressure ventilated. fluorescent lighting. B5 bogies. ETH 4X. 35 t.

80425	**RM**	E	*E*	BK
80426	**RM**	E	*E*	EN
80427	**RM**	E	*E*	EN
80428	**RM**	E	*E*	EN
80429	**RM**	E	*E*	BK
80430	**RM**	E	*E*	EN

Lot No. 30901 Wolverton 1977. converted from SK. Dia. NT521. Pressure ventilated. Fluorescent lighting. B5 bogies. ETH 4X. 35 t.

80431	(25104)	**RM**	E	*E*	EN
80432	(25071)	**RM**	E	*E*	EN
80433	(25150)	**RM**	E	*E*	BK
80434	(25119)	**RM**	E	*E*	EN
80435	(25117)	**RM**	E	*E*	EN
80436	(25077)	**RM**	E	*E*	EN
80437	(25068)	**RM**	E	*E*	EN
80438	(25139)	**RM**	E	*E*	BK
80439	(25127)	**RM**	E	*E*	BK

NU (BPOT) BRAKE POST OFFICE STOWAGE VAN

Dia. NU502. Mark 1. As NT but with brake compartment. Pressure ventilated. B5 bogies. ETH4.

Lot No. 30782 York 1968. 36 t.

80456	**RM**	E	*E*	EN
80457	**RM**	E	*E*	EN
80458	**RM**	E	*E*	EN

ND (BG) GANGWAYED BRAKE VAN (90 m.p.h.)

Dia. ND501. Mark 1. Short frames (57'). Load 10t. All vehicles were built with BR Mark 1 bogies. ETH 1. Vehicles numbered 81xxx had 3000 added to the original numbers to avoid confusion with Class 81 locomotives. The full lot number list is listed here for reference purposes with renumbered vehicles. No unmodified vehicles remain in service.

80525. Lot No. 30009 Derby 1952–53. 31 t.
80621. Lot No. 30046 York 1954. 31.5 t.
80700. Lot No. 30136 Metro-Cammell 1955. 31.5 t.
80731–80791. Lot No. 30140 BRCW 1955–56. 31.5 t.
80826–80848. Lot No. 30144 Cravens 1955. 31.5 t.
80855–80960. Lot No. 30162 Pressed Steel 1956–57. 32 t.
80971–81014. Lot No. 30173 York 1956. 31.5 t.
81025–81051. Lot No. 30224 Cravens 1956. 31.5 t.
81055–81175. Lot No. 30228 Metro-Cammell 1957–58. 31.5 t.
81182–81188. Lot No. 30234 Cravens 1956–57. 31.5 t.
81205–81265. Lot No. 30163 Pressed Steel 1957. 31.5 t.
81266–81309. Lot No. 30323 Pressed Steel 1957. 32 t.
81316–81497. Lot No. 30400 Pressed Steel 1957–58. 32 t.
81498–81568. Lot No. 30484 Pressed Steel 1958. 32 t.
81590. Lot No. 30715 Gloucester 1962. 31 t.
81604–81606. Lot No. 30716 Gloucester 1962. 31 t.

The following vehicle is an ND rebogied with Commonwealth bogies and adapted for use as exhibition van 1998 at Lancastrian Carriage & Wagon Co. Ltd. 33 t.

81025	(81025, 84025)	**0**	RA	*SS*	CP

Name: 81025 VALIANT

NZ (DLV) DRIVING BRAKE VAN (110 m.p.h.)

Dia. NZ501. Mark 3B. Air conditioned. T4 bogies. dg. ETH 5X.

Lot No. 31042 Derby 1988. 45.18 t.

82101	**V**	P	*VW*	OY
82102	**V**	P	*VW*	OY
82103	**V**	P	*VW*	OY
82104	**V**	P	*VW*	PC
82105	**V**	P	*VW*	PC
82106	**V**	P	*VW*	OY
82107	**V**	P	*VW*	PC
82108	**V**	P	*VW*	PC
82109	**V**	P	*VW*	PC
82110	**V**	P	*VW*	PC
82111	**V**	P	*VW*	PC
82112	**V**	P	*VW*	PC
82113	**V**	P	*VW*	OY
82114	**V**	P	*VW*	MA
82115	**V**	P	*VW*	MA
82116	**V**	P	*VW*	PC
82117	**V**	P	*VW*	PC
82118	**V**	P	*VW*	OY
82119	**V**	P	*VW*	MA
82120	**V**	P	*VW*	MA
82121	**V**	P	*VW*	PC
82122	**V**	P	*VW*	MA

82123	**V**	P	*VW*	PC
82124	**V**	P	*VW*	PC
82125	**V**	P	*VW*	PC
82126	**V**	P	*VW*	OY
82127	**V**	P	*VW*	OY
82128	**V**	P	*VW*	OY
82129	**V**	P	*VW*	OY
82130	**V**	P	*VW*	MA
82131	**V**	P	*VW*	OY
82132	**V**	P	*VW*	OY
82133	**V**	P	*VW*	OY
82134	**V**	P	*VW*	OY
82135	**V**	P	*VW*	MA
82136	**V**	P	*VW*	MA
82137	**V**	P	*VW*	MA
82138	**V**	P	*VW*	PC
82139	**V**	P	*VW*	PC
82140	**V**	P	*VW*	MA
82141	**V**	P	*VW*	MA
82142	**V**	P	*VW*	MA
82143	**V**	P	*VW*	OY
82144	**V**	P	*VW*	OY
82145	**V**	P	*VW*	MA
82146	**V**	P	*VW*	MA
82147	**V**	P	*VW*	MA
82148	**V**	P	*VW*	PC
82149	**V**	P	*VW*	PC
82150	**V**	P	*VW*	PC
82151	**V**	P	*VW*	OY
82152	**V**	P	*VW*	MA

Names:

82101	101 Squadron
82115	Liverpool John Moores University
82120	Liverpool Chamber of Commerce
82121	Carlisle Cathedral
82124	The Girls' Brigade
82126	G8 Summit Birmingham 1998
82127	Abraham Darby
82132	INDUSTRY 96 West Mid!ands
82134	Sir Henry Doulton 1820–1897
82135	Spirit of Cumbria
82147	The Red Devils
82148	International Spring Fair

NZ (DLV) DRIVING BRAKE VAN (140 m.p.h.)

Dia. NZ502. Mark 4. Air conditioned. Swiss-built (SIG) bogies. dg. ETH 6X.

Lot No. 31043 Metro-Cammell 1988. 45.18 t.

82200	**GN**	H		ZC
82201	**GN**	H	*GN*	BN
82202	**GN**	H	*GN*	BN
82203	**GN**	H	*GN*	BN
82204	**GN**	H	*GN*	BN
82205	**GN**	H	*GN*	BN
82206	**GN**	H	*GN*	BN
82207	**GN**	H	*GN*	BN
82208	**GN**	H	*GN*	BN
82209	**GN**	H	*GN*	BN
82210	**GN**	H	*GN*	BN
82211	**GN**	H	*GN*	BN
82212	**GN**	H	*GN*	BN
82213	**GN**	H	*GN*	BN
82214	**GN**	H	*GN*	BN
82215	**GN**	H	*GN*	BN
82216	**GN**	H	*GN*	BN
82217	**GN**	H	*GN*	BN
82218	**GN**	H	*GN*	BN
82219	**GN**	H	*GN*	BN
82220	**GN**	H	*GN*	BN
82221	**GN**	H		ZF
82222	**GN**	H	*GN*	BN
82223	**GN**	H	*GN*	BN
82224	**GN**	H	*GN*	BN
82225	**GN**	H	*GN*	BN
82226	**GN**	H	*GN*	BN
82227	**GN**	H	*GN*	BN
82228	**GN**	H	*GN*	BN
82229	**GN**	H	*GN*	BN
82230	**GN**	H	*GN*	BN
82231	**GN**	H	*GN*	BN

NJ (GUV) GENERAL UTILITY VAN

Dia. NJ501. Mark 1. Short frames. Load 14 t. Screw couplings. These vehicles had 7000 added to the original numbers to avoid confusion with Class 86 locomotives. The full lot number list is listed here for reference purposes with renumbered vehicles. No unmodified vehicles remain in service. All vehicles were built with BR Mark 2 bogies. ETH 0 or 0X*.

86081–86499. Lot No. 30417 Pressed Steel 1958–59. 30 t.
86508–86518. Lot No. 30343 York 1957. 30 t.
86521–86651. Lot No. 30403 York/Glasgow 1958–60. 30 t.
86656–86834. Lot No. 30565 Pressed Steel 1959. 30 t.
86836–86978. Lot No. 30616 Pressed Steel 1959–60. 30 t.

NE/NH (BG) GANGWAYED BRAKE VAN (100/110 m.p.h.)

NE are ND but rebogied with B4 bogies suitable for 100 m.p.h. NH are identical but are allowed to run at 110 m.p.h. with special maintenance of the bogies. For lot numbers refer to original number series. Deduct 1.5t from weights. All NHA are *pg. ETH 1 (1X*).

Non-standard Livery: 92116 is purple.

84387	(81387, 80461)	x	**B**	E		CW
84477	(81477, 80463)	x	**B**	E		CW
92100	(81391)	to		RV		CP
92111	(81432)	NHA		H		CP
92114	(81443)	NHA		H		LT
92116	(81450)	to	**0**	RK		DY
92125	(81470)	to		DR		KM
92146	(81498)	NHA		H		LT
92159	(81534)	NHA		H	*VL*	CF
92174	(81567)	NHA		H		PY
92175	(81568)	pg		H		CP
92193	(81604)	pg		E		PR
92194	(81606)	to		H		PY
92234	(81336, 84336)	*	**RX**	E		DY
92238	(81563, 84563)		**RY**	E		DY
92261	(80988)	x*	**RY**	E		BK

NE (BG) GANGWAYED BRAKE VAN (100 m.p.h.)

As ND but rebogied with Commonwealth bogies suitable for 100 m.p.h. ETH 1 (1X*). For lot numbers refer to original number series. Add 1.5 t to weights to allow for the increased weight of the Commonwealth bogies.

92302	(81501, 84501)		**RX**	E	ZG
92303	(81427, 84427)		**RX**	E	DY
92306	(81217, 84217)	*	**RY**	E	HY
92309	(81043, 84043)	x*	**RX**	E	Arpley Yard
92311	(81453, 84453)	x	**RY**	E	CW
92312	(81548, 84548)		**RX**	E	CL

92314	(80777)	x*	RY	E	CW
92316	(80980)	x*	RY	E	ZG
92319	(81055, 84055)	*	RY	E	CL
92321	(81566, 84566)		RY	E	FP
92323	(80832)	*	R	E	CL
92324	(81087, 84087)		RY	E	CL
92325	(80791)		RY	E	HY
92328	(80999)	x*	RY	E	ZG
92329	(81001, 84001)	*	RY	E	ZG
92330	(80995)	x*	RY	E	ZG
92332	(80845)	*	RX	E	CL
92333	(80982)	*	RY	E	HY
92337	(81140, 84140)	*	RX	E	CL
92340	(81059, 84059)	*	RY	E	CL
92341	(81316, 84316)	x	RY	E	HY
92343	(81505, 84505)	x	R	E	CL
92344	(81154, 84154)	*	RY	E	ZG
92345	(81083, 84083)	x*	RY	E	ZG
92346	(81091, 84091)		RY	E	OM
92347	(81326, 84326)		RX	E	DY
92348	(81075, 84075)	x*	R	E	CL
92350	(81049, 84049)	*	RY	E	DY
92353	(81323, 84323)		R	E	HY
92355	(81517, 84517)	x	RX	E	DY
92356	(81535, 84535)	x		E	OM
92357	(81136, 84136)		RX	E	HY
92362	(81188, 84188)	x	RY	E	CL
92363	(81294, 84294)	x	RY	E	CW
92364	(81030, 84030)	x*	R	E	CL
92365	(81122, 84122)		RX	E	CL
92366	(81551, 84551)		RX	E	CL
92369	(80960)	x*		E	ZF
92370	(81324, 84324)		RX	E	ZG
92377	(80928)	*	RX	E	DY
92379	(80914)	*	RX	E	CL
92380	(81247, 84247)	*	R	E	CL
92381	(81476, 84476)		RX	E	OM
92382	(81561, 84561)		RX	E	DY
92384	(80893)		RY	E	CW
92385	(81261, 84261)	x*	RY	E	CL
92389	(81026, 84026)	*	RY	E	ZG
92390	(80834)	*		E	CL
92392	(80861)	*	RY	E	ZG
92395	(81274, 84274)			E	CL
92398	(80859)	x*	RY	E	CL
92400	(81211, 84211)	*		E	CW
92401	(81280, 84280)	x	RX	E	HY
92402	(81099, 84099)	*	RY	E	HY
92404	(81051, 84051)	x		E	CL
92410	(81469, 84469)	x		E	CW
92412	(81354, 84354)	*	RY	E	CW

92413	(81472, 84472)	x	**RY**	E		CW
92415	(81388, 84388)		**RX**	E		CL
92416	(81250, 84250)	*	**RY**	E		OM
92417	(80885)	*	**RX**	E		CL

NB HIGH SECURITY BRAKE VAN (100 m.p.h.)

Dia. NB501. Mark 1. Converted from ND at Wembley Heavy Repair Depot in 1985. Gangways removed. Now used for movement of materials between EWS maintenance depots. B4 bogies.

92530	(81461, 84461)	x	**RX**	E	*E*	EN

NF (BG) GANGWAYED BRAKE VAN (100 m.p.h.)

As NE but with emergency equipment removed. For details and lot numbers refer to original number series. 92542 has B4 bogies whilst the rest have Commonwealth bogies.

92542	(81207, 92942)		**RX**	E	CL
92804	(81339, 92304)	x	**RX**	E	ZG
92805	(81590, 92305)	x	**RX**	E	CL
92810	(81105, 92310)		**RX**	E	CL
92815	(80848, 92315)	*	**RX**	E	CU
92817	(80836, 92317)	x	**RX**	E	CL
92822	(80771, 92322)	x	**RX**	E	Arpley Yard
92827	(80842, 92327)	x	**RX**	E	CL
92831	(81365, 92331)	x	**RX**	E	OM
92842	(81397, 92342)	x	**RY**	E	OM
92852	(81182, 92352)	*	**RX**	E	DY
92854	(81353, 92354)	x	**RX**	E	Arpley Yard
92859	(81275, 92359)	*	**RX**	E	DY
92860	(81431, 92360)		**RX**	E	ZG
92861	(81463, 92361)		**R**	E	CL
92867	(81293, 92367)	x	**RX**	E	CU
92872	(81362, 92372)	x	**RY**	E	CW
92873	(81528, 92373)		**RX**	E	HY
92876	(81374, 92376)	*	**RX**	E	CL
92886	(80843, 92386)	x	**RX**	E	CL
92897	(80700, 92397)	x*	**RY**	E	ZG

NE/NH (BG) GANGWAYED BRAKE VAN (100/110 m.p.h.)

Renumbered from 920xx series by adding 900 to number to avoid conflict with Class 92 locos. Class continued from 92261.

92901	(80855, 92001)	NHA		H		PY
92904	(80867, 92004)	*pg	**G**	VS		SL
92908	(80895, 92008)	NHA		H	*VL*	CF
92912	(80910, 92012)	*pg		H		KT
92923	(80971, 92023)	*pg		H		LT
92927	(81061, 92027)	NHA		H		LT

92928	(81064, 92028)	NHA	H	LT
92929	(81077, 92029)	NHA	LW	CP
92931	(81102, 92031)	NHA	H	PY
92933	(81123, 92033)	NHA	H	NC
92934	(81142, 92034)	NHA	H	LT
92935	(81150, 92035)	*pg	H	PY
92936	(81158, 92036)	NHA	H	CP
92937	(81165, 92037)	NHA	H	LT
92938	(81173, 92038)	NHA	H	PY
92939	(81175, 92039)	NHA	H	LT
92940	(81186, 92040)	pg	H	IS
92946	(81214, 92046)	NHA	H	PY
92948	(81218, 92048)	NHA	H	PY
92961	(81231, 92061)		H	LT
92986	(81282, 92086)	to	H	CP
92988	(81284, 92088)	to	H	LT
92991	(81308, 92091)	to	H	LT
92998	(81381, 92098)	NHA	H	LT

NL NEWSPAPER VAN

Dia. NL501. Mark 1. Short frames (57'). Converted from NJ (GUV). Fluorescent lighting, toilets and gangways fitted. Load 14 t. All except 94003/6, now used for materials storage, are out of use. B5 Bogies. ETH 3X.

Lot No. 30922 Wolverton or Doncaster 1977–78. 31 t.

94003	(86281, 93999)	x	**RX**	GW	*GW*	OO
94004	(86156, 85504)		**RY**	E		OM
94006	(86202, 85506)		**RX**	GW	*GW*	OO
94007	(86572, 85507)		**B**	E		OM
94009	(86144, 85509)		**RY**	E		OM
94016	(86317, 85516)	x	**B**	E		OM
94020	(86220, 85520)	x	**RY**	E		OM
94021	(86204, 85521)	x	**B**	E		OM
94026	(86703, 85526)	x	**RY**	E		OM
94027	(86732, 85527)		**R**	E		FP
94029	(86740, 85529)	x	**RY**	E		OM
94030	(86746, 85530)	x	**B**	E		OM

NKA HIGH SECURITY GENERAL UTILITY VAN

Dia. NK501. Mark 1. These vehicles are GUVs further modified with new floors, three roller shutter doors per side and the end doors removed. For lot Nos. see original number series. Commonwealth bogies. Add 2 t to weight. ETH0X.

94100	(86668, 95100)	**RX**	E	*E*	BK
94101	(86142, 95101)	**RX**	E	*E*	BK
94102	(86762, 95102)	**RX**	E	*E*	BK
94103	(86956, 95103)	**RX**	E	*E*	BK
94104	(86942, 95104)	**RX**	E	*E*	EN
94106	(86353, 95106)	**RX**	E	*E*	BK

94107	(86576, 95107)	**RX**	E	*E*	EN
94108	(86600, 95108)	**RX**	E	*E*	BK
94110	(86393, 95110)	**RX**	E	*E*	BK
94111	(86578, 95111)	**RX**	E	*E*	EN
94112	(86673, 95112)	**RX**	E	*E*	EN
94113	(86235, 95113)	**RX**	E	*E*	BK
94114	(86081, 95114)	**RX**	E	*E*	BK
94116	(86426, 95116)	**RX**	E	*E*	BK
94117	(86534, 95117)	**RX**	E	*E*	BK
94118	(86675, 95118)	**RX**	E	*E*	EN
94119	(86167, 95119)	**RX**	E	*E*	EN
94121	(86518, 95121)	**RX**	E	*E*	BK
94123	(86376, 95123)	**RX**	E	*E*	BK
94126	(86692, 95126)	**RX**	E	*E*	BK
94132	(86607, 95132)	**RX**	E	*E*	EN
94133	(86604, 95133)	**RX**	E	*E*	BK
94137	(86610, 95137)	**RX**	E	*E*	EN
94138	(86212, 95138)	**RX**	E	*E*	EN
94140	(86571, 95140)	**RX**	E	*E*	BK
94146	(86648, 95146)	**RX**	E	*E*	BK
94147	(86091, 95147)	**RX**	E	*E*	BK
94148	(86416, 95148)	**RX**	E	*E*	EN
94150	(86560, 95150)	**RX**	E	*E*	BK
94153	(86798, 95153)	**RX**	E	*E*	EN
94155	(86820, 95155)	**RX**	E	*E*	EN
94157	(86523, 95157)	**RX**	E	*E*	EN
94160	(86581, 95160)	**RX**	E	*E*	BK
94164	(86104, 95164)	**RX**	E	*E*	EN
94166	(86112, 95166)	**RX**	E	*E*	BK
94168	(86914, 95168)	**RX**	E	*E*	BK
94170	(86395, 95170)	**RX**	E	*E*	BK
94172	(86429, 95172)	**RX**	E	*E*	EN
94174	(86852, 95174)	**RX**	E	*E*	EN
94175	(86521, 95175)	**RX**	E	*E*	BK
94176	(86210, 95176)	**RX**	E	*E*	EN
94177	(86411, 95177)	**RX**	E	*E*	BK
94180	(86362, 95141)	**RX**	E	*E*	EN
94182	(86710, 95182)	**RX**	E	*E*	BK
94190	(86624, 95350)	**RX**	E	*E*	EN
94191	(86596, 95351)	**RX**	E	*E*	BK
94192	(86727, 95352)	**RX**	E	*E*	EN
94193	(86514, 95353)	**RX**	E	*E*	EN
94195	(86375, 95355)	**RX**	E	*E*	BK
94196	(86478, 95356)	**RX**	E	*E*	BK
94197	(86508, 95357)	**RX**	E	*E*	BK
94198	(86195, 95358)	**RX**	E	*E*	BK
94199	(86854, 95359)	**RX**	E	*E*	BK
94200	(86207, 95360)	**RX**	E	*E*	EN
94202	(86563, 95362)	**RX**	E	*E*	BK
94203	(86345, 95363)	**RX**	E	*E*	BK
94204	(86715, 95364)	**RX**	E	*E*	BK

94205	(86857, 95365)	**RX**	E	*E*	BK
94207	(86529, 95367)	**RX**	E	*E*	BK
94208	(86656, 95368)	**RX**	E	*E*	EN
94209	(86390, 95369)	**RX**	E	*E*	BK
94211	(86713, 95371)	**RX**	E	*E*	EN
94212	(86728, 95372)	**RX**	E	*E*	EN
94213	(86258, 95373)	**RX**	E	*E*	EN
94214	(86367, 95374)	**RX**	E	*E*	BK
94215	(86862, 94077)	**RX**	E	*E*	BK
94216	(86711, 93711)	**RX**	E	*E*	EN
94217	(86131, 93131)	**RX**	E	*E*	BK
94218	(86541, 93541)	**RX**	E	*E*	BK
94221	(86905, 93905)	**RX**	E	*E*	BK
94222	(86474, 93474)	**RX**	E	*E*	EN
94223	(86660, 93660)	**RX**	E	*E*	BK
94224	(86273, 93273)	**RX**	E	*E*	BK
94225	(86849, 93849)	**RX**	E	*E*	BK
94226	(86525, 93525)	**RX**	E	*E*	BK
94227	(86585, 93585)	**RX**	E	*E*	BK
94228	(86511, 93511)	**RX**	E	*E*	BK
94229	(86720, 93720)	**RX**	E	*E*	BK

NAA PROPELLING CONTROL VEHICLE

Dia. NA508. Mark 1. Class 307 driving trailers converted for use in propelling mail trains out of termini. Fitted with roller shutter doors. Equipment fitted for communication between cab of PCV and locomotive. B5 bogies. ETH 2X.

Lot No. 30206 Eastleigh 1954–56. Converted at Hunslet-Barclay, Kilmarnock 1994–6.

94302	(75124)	**RX**	E	*E*	BK
94303	(75131)	**RX**	E	*E*	EN
94304	(75107)	**RX**	E	*E*	EN
94305	(75104)	**RX**	E	*E*	EN
94306	(75112)	**RX**	E	*E*	BK
94307	(75127)	**RX**	E	*E*	EN
94308	(75125)	**RX**	E	*E*	EN
94309	(75130)	**RX**	E	*E*	EN
94310	(75119)	**RX**	E	*E*	EN
94311	(75105)	**RX**	E	*E*	EN
94312	(75126)	**RX**	E	*E*	BK
94313	(75129)	**RX**	E	*E*	BK
94314	(75109)	**RX**	E	*E*	BK
94315	(75132)	**RX**	E	*E*	EN
94316	(75108)	**RX**	E	*E*	EN
94317	(75117)	**RX**	E	*E*	EN
94318	(75115)	**RX**	E	*E*	EN
94319	(75128)	**RX**	E	*E*	EN
94320	(75120)	**RX**	E	*E*	EN
94321	(75122)	**RX**	E	*E*	EN
94322	(75111)	**RX**	E	*E*	BK
94323	(75110)	**RX**	E	*E*	EN
94324	(75103)	**RX**	E	*E*	EN
94325	(75113)	**RX**	E	*E*	EN
94326	(75123)	**RX**	E	*E*	BK
94327	(75116)	**RX**	E	*E*	EN
94331	(75022)	**RX**	E	*E*	BK
94332	(75011)	**RX**	E	*E*	EN
94333	(75016)	**RX**	E	*E*	EN
94334	(75017)	**RX**	E	*E*	EN
94335	(75032)	**RX**	E	*E*	BK
94336	(75031)	**RX**	E	*E*	EN
94337	(75029)	**RX**	E	*E*	EN
94338	(75008)	**RX**	E	*E*	EN
94339	(75024)	**RX**	E	*E*	BK
94340	(75012)	**RX**	E	*E*	BK
94341	(75007)	**RX**	E	*E*	BK
94342	(75005)	**RX**	E	*E*	BK
94343	(75027)	**RX**	E	*E*	EN
94344	(75014)	**RX**	E	*E*	BK
94345	(75004)	**RX**	E	*E*	EN

NBA HIGH SECURITY BRAKE VAN (100 m.p.h.)

Dia. NB501. Mark 1. These vehicles are NEs further modified with sealed gangways, new floors, built-in tail lights and roller shutter doors. For lot Nos. see original number series. B4 bogies. 31.4 t. ETH 1X.

94400	(81224, 92954)	**RX**	E	*E*	BK
94401	(81277, 92224)	**RX**	E	*E*	EN
94403	(81479, 92629)	**RX**	E	*E*	BK
94404	(81486, 92135)	**RX**	E	*E*	BK
94405	(80890, 92233)	**RX**	E	*E*	EN
94406	(81226, 92956)	**RX**	E	*E*	BK
94407	(81223, 92553)	**RX**	E	*E*	BK
94408	(81264, 92981)	**RX**	E	*E*	BK
94410	(81205, 92941)	**RX**	E	*E*	EN
94411	(81378, 92997)	**RX**	E	*E*	EN
94412	(81210, 92945)	**RX**	E	*E*	EN
94413	(80909, 92236)	**RX**	E	*E*	EN
94414	(81377, 92996)	**RX**	E	*E*	BK
94415	(81309, 92992)	**RX**	E	*E*	EN
94416	(80929, 92746)	**RX**	E	*E*	BK
94418	(81248, 92244)	**RX**	E	*E*	BK
94420	(81325, 92263)	**RX**	E	*E*	BK
94422	(81516, 92651)	**RX**	E	*E*	BK
94423	(80923, 92914)	**RX**	E	*E*	BK
94424	(81400, 92103)	**RX**	E	*E*	EN
94427	(80894, 92754)	**RX**	E	*E*	BK
94428	(81550, 92166)	**RX**	E	*E*	BK
94429	(80870, 92232)	**RX**	E	*E*	EN
94431	(81401, 92604)	**RX**	E	*E*	BK
94432	(81383, 92999)	**RX**	E	*E*	EN
94433	(81495, 92643)	**RX**	E	*E*	EN
94434	(81268, 92584)	**RX**	E	*E*	EN
94435	(81485, 92134)	**RX**	E	*E*	EN
94436	(81237, 92565)	**RX**	E	*E*	BK
94437	(81403, 92208)	**RX**	E	*E*	EN
94438	(81425, 92251)	**RX**	E	*E*	BK
94439	(81480, 92130)	**RX**	E	*E*	BK
94440	(81497, 92645)	**RX**	E	*E*	BK
94441	(81492, 92140)	**RX**	E	*E*	BK
94442	(80932, 92723)	**RX**	E	*E*	BK
94443	(81473, 92127)	**RX**	E	*E*	BK
94444	(81484, 92133)	**RX**	E	*E*	BK
94445	(81444, 92615)	**RX**	E	*E*	EN
94446	(80857, 92242)	**RX**	E	*E*	EN
94447	(81515, 92266)	**RX**	E	*E*	EN
94448	(81541, 92664)	**RX**	E	*E*	BK
94449	(81536, 92747)	**RX**	E	*E*	BK
94450	(80927, 92915)	**RX**	E	*E*	BK
94451	(80955, 92257)	**RX**	E	*E*	EN

94452	(81394, 92602)	**RX**	E	*E*	BK
94453	(81170, 92239)	**RX**	E	*E*	EN
94454	(81465, 92124)	**RX**	E	*E*	EN
94455	(81239, 92264)	**RX**	E	*E*	BK
94458	(81255, 92974)	**RX**	E	*E*	BK
94459	(81490, 92138)	**RX**	E	*E*	BK
94460	(81266, 92983)	**RX**	E	*E*	EN
94461	(81487, 92136)	**RX**	E	*E*	EN
94462	(81289, 92270)	**RX**	E	*E*	EN
94463	(81375, 92995)	**RX**	E	*E*	EN
94464	(81240, 92262)	**RX**	E	*E*	EN
94465	(81481, 92131)	**RX**	E	*E*	BK
94466	(81236, 92964)	**RX**	E	*E*	EN
94467	(81245, 92969)	**RX**	E	*E*	BK
94468	(81259, 92978)	**RX**	E	*E*	BK
94469	(81260, 92979)	**RX**	E	*E*	BK
94470	(81442, 92113)	**RX**	E	*E*	EN
94471	(81518, 92152)	**RX**	E	*E*	BK
94472	(81256, 92975)	**RX**	E	*E*	BK
94473	(81262, 92272)	**RX**	E	*E*	EN
94474	(81452, 92618)	**RX**	E	*E*	EN
94475	(81208, 92943)	**RX**	E	*E*	EN
94476	(81209, 92944)	**RX**	E	*E*	BK
94477	(81494, 92642)	**RX**	E	*E*	BK
94478	(81488, 92637)	**RX**	E	*E*	EN
94479	(81482, 92132)	**RX**	E	*E*	BK
94480	(81411, 92608)	**RX**	E	*E*	EN
94481	(81493, 92641)	**RX**	E	*E*	BK
94482	(81491, 92639)	**RX**	E	*E*	EN
94483	(81500, 92647)	**RX**	E	*E*	EN
94484	(81426, 92110)	**RX**	E	*E*	BK
94485	(81496, 92644)	**RX**	E	*E*	EN
94486	(81254, 92973)	**RX**	E	*E*	BK
94487	(81413, 92609)	**RX**	E	*E*	BK
94488	(81405, 92105)	**RX**	E	*E*	BK
94490	(81409, 92606)	**RX**	E	*E*	EN
94492	(80888, 92721)	**RX**	E	*E*	BK
94493	(80944, 92919)	**RX**	E	*E*	BK
94494	(81451, 92617)	**RX**	E	*E*	BK
94495	(80871, 92755)	**RX**	E	*E*	BK
94496	(81514, 92650)	**RX**	E	*E*	BK
94497	(80877, 92717)	**RX**	E	*E*	BK
94498	(81225, 92555)	**RX**	E	*E*	BK
94499	(81258, 92577)	**RX**	E	*E*	BK

NBA/NIA/NQA HIGH SECURITY BRAKE VAN

Dia. NB501, NI501 or NQ501. Mark 1. These vehicles are NEs further modified with sealed gangways, new floors, built-in tail lights and roller shutter doors. For lot Nos. see original number series. B4 bogies. 31.4 t. ETH 1X.

▲ **Mark 3 (HST) Stock.** Trailer standard buffet (TRSB) 40416 in Virgin livery at Reading on 21/06/2001 in the formation of the 12.20 Bournemouth–Edinburgh.
Kevin Conkey

▼ Open first (FO) 41033 in Great Western livery at Reading on the same day in the 12.55 Cardiff–London Paddington.
Kevin Conkey

Mark 3B Loco-hauled Stock. BFO 17174, one of three brake open firsts built for the first-class only Manchester Pullman service. By the time they had been delivered this train had changed to a normal first and standard class formation. The coach is in the formation of the 14.33 London Euston–Glasgow Central at Milton Keynes on 09/06/2000. **Mark Beal**

Mark 4 Stock. Restauranr Buffet first (RFM0 10312 at London Kings Cross on 19/06/2001 in the 12.40 ex-Leeds.
Kevin Conkey

▲ Mark 4 Driving Van Trailer (DVT) 82226 at London Kings Cross on 19/06/2001 in the 13.15 ex-York. **Kevin Conkey**

▼ Post Office Control Vehicle (PCV) 94325 at Plymouth Station on 30/05/2001. **Allan Brooks**

▲ Post Office Stowage Van (POT) 80406 at Plymouth on 28/05/2001.
Stephen Widdowson

▲ NKA (High Security General Utility Van) 95734 at Carlisle on 20/07/2001.
Kevin Conkey

First Great Western Motorail Van 96606 at London Paddington on 22/08/2000. **Mark Beal**

LMS "Club Car" 99993, part of the 'Queen of Scots' Pullman train at the EWS Old Oak Common open day on 05/08/2000.
A. Milliken

EWS Match vehicle DB 977949 at Carlisle on 24/05/2001at the back of a set of Class 334s being delivered to Glasgow.
Kevin Conkey

These vehicles are identical to the 94400–94499 series. Certain vehicles are being given a special maintenance regime whereby tyres are reprofiled more frequently than normal and are then allowed to run at 110 m.p.h. Vehicles from the 94400 series upgraded to 110 m.p.h. are being renumbered in this series. Vehicles are NBA (100 m.p.h.) unless marked NIA (110 m.p.h. not to be hauled by Class 90/2 locomotives) or NQA (110 m.p.h. suitable for haulage by Class 90/2 locomotive.

94500	(81457, 92121)	NIA	**RX**	E	*E*	ML
94501	(80891, 92725)		**RX**	E	*E*	BK
94502	(80924, 92720)	NQA	**RX**	E	*E*	ML
94503	(80873, 92709)	NIA	**RX**	E	*E*	ML
94504	(80935, 92748)	NQA	**RX**	E	*E*	BK
94505	(81235, 92750)	NIA	**RX**	E	*E*	ML
94506	(80958, 92922)	NIA	**RX**	E	*E*	ML
94507	(80876, 92505)	NIA	**RX**	E	*E*	ML
94508	(80887, 92722)	NQA	**RX**	E	*E*	ML
94509	(80897, 92509)	NQA	**RX**	E	*E*	ML
94510	(80945, 92265)		**RX**	E	*E*	BK
94511	(81504, 92714)	NIA	**RX**	E	*E*	ML
94512	(81265, 92582)		**RX**	E	*E*	BK
94513	(81257, 92576)		**RX**	E	*E*	BK
94514	(81459, 92122)	NIA	**RX**	E	*E*	ML
94515	(80916, 92513)	NQA	**RX**	E	*E*	ML
94516	(81267, 92211)	NQA	**RX**	E	*E*	ML
94517	(81489, 92243)	NIA	**RX**	E	*E*	BK
94518	(81346, 92258)		**RX**	E	*E*	BK
94519	(80930, 92916)	NQA	**RX**	E	*E*	ML
94520	(80940, 92917)	NQA	**RX**	E	*E*	ML
94521	(80900, 92510)	NIA	**RX**	E	*E*	ML
94522	(80880, 92907)	NIA	**RX**	E	*E*	ML
94523	(81509, 92649)	NIA	**RX**	E	*E*	BK
94524	(81454, 94457)	NQA	**RX**	E	*E*	ML
94525	(80902, 92229)	NIA	**RX**	E	*E*	ML
94526	(80941, 92518)	NIA	**RX**	E	*E*	ML
94527	(80924, 92728)	NQA	**RX**	E	*E*	ML
94528	(81404, 92267)		**RX**	E	*E*	BK
94529	(80959, 92252)	NQA	**RX**	E	*E*	ML
94530	(81511, 94409)	NIA	**RX**	E	*E*	ML
94531	(80879, 94456)	NQA	**RX**	E	*E*	ML
94532	(81423, 94489)	NQA	**RX**	E	*E*	BK
94533	(80937, 94425)	NIA	**RX**	E	*E*	BK
94534	(80908, 94430)	NIA	**RX**	E	*E*	BK
94535	(80858, 94419)	NIA	**RX**	E	*E*	BK
94536	(80936, 94491)	NIA	**RX**	E	*E*	BK
94537	(81230, 94421)	NIA	**RX**	E	*E*	BK
94538	(81283, 94426)	NQA	**RX**	E	*E*	ML

NBA HIGH SECURITY BRAKE VAN (100 m.p.h.)

Dia. NB501. Mark 1. Details as for 94400–99 but fitted with Commonwealth bogies. 34.4 t. ETH 1X.

These vehicles are identical to the 94400–94499 series. Certain vehicles are being given a special maintenance regime whereby tyres are reprofiled more frequently than normal and are then allowed to run at 110 m.p.h. Vehicles from the 94400 series upgraded to 110 m.p.h. are being renumbered in this series. Vehicles are NBA (100 m.p.h.) unless marked NIA (110 m.p.h. not to be hauled by Class 90/2 locos) or NQA (110 m.p.h. suitable for haulage by Class 90/2 locos).

94539	(81501, 92302)	E
94540	(81431, 92860)	E
94541	(80980, 92316)	E
94542	(80995, 92330)	E
94543	(81026, 92389)	E
94544	(81083, 92345)	E
94545	(81001, 92327)	E
94546	(81339, 92804)	E
94547	(80861, 92392)	E
94548	(81154, 92344)	E

NO (GUV) GENERAL UTILITY VAN (100 m.p.h.)

Dia. NO513. Mark 1. For lot Nos. see original number series. Commonwealth bogies. Add 2 t to weight. ETH 0X.

95105	(86126, 93126)		**RX**	E	CU
95109	(86269, 93269)	x	**B**	E	CU
95120	(86468, 93468)	x	**RY**	E	CU
95124	(86836, 93836)	x	**R**	E	CU
95125	(86143, 93143)	x	**B**	E	CU
95128	(86764, 93764)	x	**RY**	E	CW
95129	(86347, 93347)	x	**RY**	E	CW
95135	(86249, 93249)	x	**RY**	E	CU
95145	(86293, 93293)	x	**RX**	E	CU
95152	(86969, 93969)	x	**RY**	E	CU
95165	(86262, 93262)	x	**RX**	E	CU

NCX NEWSPAPER VAN (100 m.p.h.)

Dia. NC501. Mark 1. BGs modified to carry newspapers. As EWS does not now carry newspaper traffic these are now all out of use. For lot Nos. refer to original number series. Commonwealth bogies. Add 2 t to weight. ETH3.

95201	(80875)	x	**RX**	E	OM
95211	(80949)	x	**RY**	E	CL
95227	(81292, 95310)	x	**RX**	E	HY
95228	(81014, 95332)	x	**RX**	E	NC
95230	(80525, 95321)	x	**RX**	E	DY

NAA PROPELLING CONTROL VEHICLE

Dia. NA508. Mark 1. Class 307 driving trailers converted for use in propelling mail trains out of termini. Fitted with roller shutter doors. Equipment was fitted for communication between cab of PCV and locomotive but this is now isolated.

ETH 2X.

Lot No. 30206 Eastleigh 1954–56. Converted at RTC, Derby 1993.

95300	(75114, 94300)	**E**	E	*E*	ML
95301	(75102, 94301)	**E**	E	*E*	ML

NRX BAA CONTAINER VAN (100 m.p.h.)

Dia. NR503. Mark 1. Modified for carriage of British Airports Authority containers with roller shutter doors and roller floors and gangways removed. Now used for general parcels traffic. For lot Nos. see original number series. Commonwealth bogies. Add 2 t to weight. ETH3.

95400	(80621, 95203)	x	**E**	E	*E*	ML
95410	(80826, 95213)	x	**E**	E	*E*	ML

NKA HIGH SECURITY GENERAL UTILITY VAN

Dia. NK502. Mark 1. These vehicles are GUVs further modified with new floors, two roller shutter doors per side, middle doors sealed and end doors removed. For lot Nos. see original number series. Commonwealth bogies. Add 2 t to weight. ETH 0X.

95715	(86174, 95115)	**R**	E	*E*	EN
95727	(86323, 95127)	**R**	E	*E*	EN
95734	(86462, 95134)	**RX**	E	*E*	EN
95739	(86172, 95139)	**R**	E	*E*	EN
95743	(86485, 95143)	**RX**	E	*E*	EN
95749	(86265, 95149)	**R**	E	*E*	EN
95754	(86897, 95154)	**R**	E	*E*	EN
95758	(86499, 95158)	**RX**	E	*E*	EN
95759	(86084, 95159)	**RX**	E	*E*	EN
95761	(86205, 95161)	**RX**	E	*E*	EN
95762	(86122, 95162)	**RX**	E	*E*	EN
95763	(86407, 95163)	**R**	E	*E*	EN

NX/NV (GUV) MOTORAIL VAN (100 m.p.h.)

Dia. NX501. Mark 1. For details and lot numbers see original number series. ETH 0 (0X*).

Note: 96101 has a new prototype body built 1998 by Marcroft Engineering with side loading and one end sealed (Dia. NV501).

96100	(86734, 93734)	*B5		H	KT
96101	(86741, 93741)	*B5	**HB**	H	PY
96110	(86738, 93738)	*C		H	PY
96112	(86750, 93750)	*C		H	LT
96130	(86736, 93736)	*C		H	KT
96131	(86737, 93737)	*C		H	KT
96132	(86754, 93754)	*C		H	LT
96133	(86685, 93685)	C		H	LT
96134	(86691, 93691)	C		H	LT

96135	(86755, 93755)	C		H		CP
96136	(86735, 93735)	C		H		LT
96137	(86748, 93748)	C	**B**	H		ZN
96139	(86751, 93751)	C		H	*VW*	MA
96162	(86647, 93647)	*C		H		LT
96163	(86646, 93646)	*C		H		KT
96164	(86880, 93880)	*C		H		LT
96165	(86784, 93784)	*C		H		KT
96166	(86834, 93834)	*C		H		KT
96167	(86756, 93756)	*C		H		KT
96168	(86978, 93978)	*C		H		LT
96170	(86159, 93159)	x*C		H		KT
96171	(86326, 93326)	x*C		H		LT
96172	(86363, 93363)	x*C		H		KT
96173	(86440, 93440)	x*C		H		KT
96174	(86453, 93453)	x*C		H		LT
96175	(86628, 93628)	x*C		H		KT
96176	(86641, 93641)	x*C		H		KT
96178	(86782, 93782)	*C		H		KT
96179	(86910, 93910)	*C		H		LT
96181	(86875, 93875)	*C		H		LT
96182	(86944, 93944)	*C		H		CP
96185	(86083, 93083)	x*C		H		LT
96186	(86087, 93087)	x*C		H		LT
96187	(86168, 93168)	x*C		H		LT
96188	(86320, 93320)	x*C		H		KT
96189	(86447, 93447)	x*C		H		LT
96190	(86448, 93448)	x*C		H		LT
96191	(86665, 93665)	x*C		H		KT
96192	(86669, 93669)	x*C		H		KT
96193	(86874, 93874)	x*C		H		LT
96194	(86949, 93949)	x*C		H		LT
96195	(86958, 93958)	x*C		H		LT

NP (GUV) MOTORAIL VAN (110 m.p.h.)

Dia. NP503. Mark 1. Vehicles modified with concertina end doors. For details and lot numbers see original number series. B5 Bogies. ETH 0X.

96210	(86355, 96159)	H	LT
96212	(86443, 96161)	H	LT
96218	(86286, 96151)	H	LT

AX5G NIGHTSTAR GENERATOR VAN

Dia. AX502. Mark 3A. Generator vans converted from sleeping cars for use on 'Nightstar' services. Designed to operate between two Class 37/6 locomotives. Gangways removed. Two Cummins diesel generator groups providing a 1500 V train supply. Hydraulic parking brake. 61-way ENS interface jumpers. BT10 bogies.

Lot No. 30960 Derby 1981–83. 46.01 t.

96371	(10545, 6371)	**EP**	EU	*EU*	NP
96372	(10564, 6372)	**EP**	EU	*EU*	NP
96373	(10568, 6373)	**EP**	EU	*EU*	NP
96374	(10585, 6374)	**EP**	EU	*EU*	NP
96375	(10587, 6375)	**EP**	EU	*EU*	NP

AY5 (BV) EUROSTAR BARRIER VEHICLE

Dia. AY501. Mark 1. Converted from GUVs. Bodies removed. B4 bogies.

96380–96382/9. Lot No. 30417 Pressed Steel 1958–59. 40 t.
96383. Lot No. 30565 Pressed Steel 1959. 40 t.
96384/6/7. Lot No. 30616 Pressed Steel 1959–60. 40 t.
96385. Lot No. 30343 York 1957. 40 t.
96388. Lot No. 30403 Glasgow 1958–60. 40 t.

96380	(86386, 6380)	**B**	EU	*EU*	NP
96381	(86187, 6381)	**B**	EU	*EU*	NP
96382	(86295, 6382)	**B**	EU	*EU*	NP
96383	(86664, 6383)	**B**	EU	*EU*	NP
96384	(86955, 6384)	**B**	EU	*EU*	NP
96385	(86515, 6385)	**B**	EU	*EU*	NP
96386	(86859, 6386)	**B**	EU	*EU*	NP
96387	(86973, 6387)	**B**	EU	*EU*	NP
96388	(86562, 6388)	**B**	EU	*EU*	NP
96389	(86135, 6389)	**B**	EU	*EU*	NP

NG MOTORAIL LOADING WAGON

Dia. NG503. These vehicles have been converted and renumbered from weltrol wagons and were used for loading purposes.

Built Swindon 1960. Wagon Lot No. 3102 (3192*).

96452	(B900917)		H	LT
96453	(B900926)	*	H	LT

NVA MOTORAIL VAN (100 m.p.h.)

Dia. NV502. Mark 1. Built 1998–9 by Marcroft Engineering using underframe and running gear from Motorail GUVs. Side loading with one end sealed. The vehicles run in pairs and access is available to the adjacent vehicle. For details and lot numbers see original number series. B5 bogies. ETH 0X.

* Prototype vehicle. Dia NV501. End doors. Now out of use.

96602	(86097, 96150)	**FG**	H	*GW*	PZ
96603	(86334, 96155)	**FG**	H	*GW*	PZ
96604	(86337, 96156)	**FG**	H	*GW*	PZ
96605	(86344, 96157)	**FG**	H	*GW*	PZ
96606	(86324, 96213)	**FG**	H	*GW*	PZ
96607	(86351, 96215)	**FG**	H	*GW*	PZ
96608	(86385, 96216)	**FG**	H	*GW*	PZ
96609	(86327, 96217)	**FG**	H	*GW*	PZ

NY EXHIBITION VAN

Various interiors. Converted from various vehicle types. Electric heating from shore supply. Livery varies according to job being undertaken.

Converted Salisbury 1981 from RBs of Lot No. 30636 Pressed Steel 1962. Club cars. Dia NY523/4 respectively. Commonwealth bogies.

99645	(1765)	v **0**	E	FP
99646	(1766)	v **0**	E	FP

Converted Railway Age, Crewe 1996 from TSO to Lot No. 30822 Derby 1971. B4 bogies.

99662	(5689,)	**0**	RK	DY

Converted Railway Age, Crewe 1996 from SO to Lot No. 30821 Derby 1971. Originally FO. B4 bogies.

99663	(3194, 6223)	**0**	RK	DY
99664	(3189, 6231)	**0**	RK	DY

Converted Railway Age, Crewe 1996 from TSO to Lot No. 30837 Derby 1972. B4 bogies.

99665	(5755,)	**0**	RK	DY

Converted Railway Age, Crewe 1996 from FO to Lot No. 30843 Derby 1972–73. B4 bogies.

99666	(3250,)	**0**	RK	DY

YR FERRY VAN

Dia. YR025. This vehicle was built to a wagon lot although the design closely resembles that of NJ except it only has two sets of doors per side. Short Frames (57'). Load 14 t. Commonwealth bogies.

Built Eastleigh 1958. Wagon Lot. No. 2849. 30 t.

889202	**PC**	VS	*ON*	SL

Name: 889202 is branded 'BAGGAGE CAR No.8'.

QSA EMU TRANSLATOR VEHICLES

These vehicles are numbered in the former BR departmental number series but are included here as they are owned by leasing companies and used by them for moving their vehicles around the national system in the same way as other vehicles included in this book. Various diagrams. Converted from Mark 1 TSO, RSOs, RUOs, BSKs and GUVs (NP/NL).

975864. Lot No. 30054 Eastleigh 1951–54. BR Mark 1 bogies.
975867. Lot No. 30014 York 1950–51. BR Mark 1 bogies.
975875. Lot No. 30143 Charles Roberts 1954–55. BR Mark 1 bogies.
975971–975978. Lot No. 30647 Wolverton 1959–61. Commonwealth bogies.
977087. Lot No. 30229 Metro-Cammell 1955–57. Commonwealth bogies.
977942/944–946/949. Lot No. 30417 Pressed Steel 1958–59. B5 bogies.
977943/947–948. Lot No. 30565 Pressed Steel 1959. B5 bogies.

975864	(3849)		H	*H*	IL
975867	(1006)		H	*H*	IL
975875	(34643)	**HB**	H	*H*	HE
975971	(1054)	**P**	P	*P*	CJ
975972	(1039)	**P**	P	*P*	CJ
975973	(1021)	**P**	P	*P*	CJ
975974	(1030)	**N**	A	*A*	IL
975975	(1042)	**P**	P	*P*	CJ
975976	(1033)		A		KT
975977	(1023)		A		KT
975978	(1025)	**N**	A	*A*	IL
977087	(34971)	**HB**	H	*H*	HE
977942	(86467, 80251)	**E**	E	*E*	CF
977943	(86718, 80252)	**E**	E	*E*	CF
977944	(86151, 94010)	**E**	E		CF
977945	(86437, 94011)	**E**	E		CF
977946	(86106, 94024)	**E**	E		CF
977947	(86730, 94032)	**E**	E		CF
977948	(86733, 94028)	**E**	E	*E*	CF
977949	(86377, 94025)	**E**	E	*E*	CF

TEST TRAIN COACHES

LABORATORY & TESTING COACHES

These coaches are used for research, development, instruction, testing and inspection on the Railtrack network. Many are fitted with sophisticated technical equipment. They are numbered in the former BR departmental number series.

Non-Standard Livery: 975000/46/76/428/547 are in BR research white and red with a grey stripe.

Laboratory Coach. Converted from BR Mark 1 RSO. Lot No. 30014 York 1950–51. B4 bogies.

975000 (1003) **0** AE ZA

Laboratory Coach. Converted from BR Mark 1 BSK. Lot No. 30021 Eastleigh 1950–52. B4 bogies.

975046 (34249) **0** AE ZA

Tribometer Driving Trailer Coach. Converted from BR Mark 1 BSK. Lot No. 30060 GRCW 1954–55. B4 bogies.

975076 (34500) **0** AE ZA

Structure Gauging Driving Trailer Coach. Converted from BR Mark 1 BSK. Lot No. 30699 Wolverton 1961–63. B4 bogies.

975081 (35313) **SO** RK *SO* ZA

Overhead Line Equipment Test Coach. Can either be locomotive hauled or included between DMU vehicles 977391/2. Converted from BR Mark 1 BSK Lot No. 30142 Gloucester 1954–5. B4 bogies.

975091 (34615) **SO** RK *SO* ZA

Structure Gauging Train Dormitory and Generator Coach. Converted from BR Mark 1 BCK Lot No. 30732 Derby 1962–4. B4 bogies.

975280 (21263) **RK** RK *SO* ZA

Test Coach. Converted from BR Mark 2 FK Lot No. 30734 Derby 1962–64. B4 bogies.

975290 (13396) **SO** SO *SO* ZA

Test Coach. Converted from BR Mark 1 BSK Lot No. 30699 Wolverton 1961–63. Commonwealth bogies.

975397 (35386) **SO** SO *SO* ZA

Test Coach. Converted from BR Mark 1 BSK Lot No. 30223 Charles Roberts 1955–56. B5 bogies.

975422 (34875) **SO** SO *SO* ZA

Laboratory/Generator Coach. Converted from BR Mark 1 BSO Lot No. 30170 Doncaster 1954–56. B4 bogies.

975428 (9236) **0** SO ZA

Laboratory/Generator Coach. Converted from BR Mark 1 BG Lot No. 30725 GRCW 1962–63. B4 bogies.

975547 (81617)	**0**	SO		ZA

Test Coach. Converted from Mark 3 TRUB Lot No. 30849 Derby 1972–3. BT10 bogies.

975984 (10000, 40000)	**SO**	SO	*SO*	ZA

High Speed Track Recording Train Generator Coach. Converted from Class 438 750 V d.c. third rail EMU driving trailer. Lot No. 30764 York 1965–67, which in turn had been converted from BR Mark 1 TSO Lot No. 30149 Swindon 1956–57. B5 (SR) bogies.

977335 (4005, 76277)	**SO**	SO	*SO*	ZA

High Speed Track Recording Train Dormitory Coach. Converted from BR Mark 2 BSO. Lot No 30757 Derby 1965–66. B4 bogies.

977337 (9395)	**SO**	SO	*SO*	ZA

High Speed Track Recording Train Brake & Stores Coach. Converted from Mark 2 BSO. Lot No. 30757 Derby 1965–66. B4 bogies.

977338 (9387)	**SO**	RK	*SO*	ZA

Laboratory Coach. Converted from BR Mark 2 TSO. Lot No. 30751 Derby 1965–67. B4 bogies.

977469 (5190)	**AE**	AE	*AE*	ZA

Test Train Staff and Dormitory Coach. Converted from BR Mark 3 SLEP. Lot No. 30960 Derby 1979–83. BT10 bogies.

977855 (10576)	**SO**	RK	*SO*	ZA

Instruction Coaches. Converted from BR Mark 2E TSO. Lot No. 30844 Derby 1972–73. B4 bogies.

977867 (5841)	**AR**	AR	*AR*	NC
977868 (5846)	**RK**	RK	*SO*	ZA
977869 (5858)	**RK**	RK	*SO*	ZA

Test Coach. Converted from BR Inspection Saloon. BR Wagon Lot No. 3095. Swindon 1957. B4 bogies.

999506		RK		ZA

Track Recording Coach. Converted from BR Inspection Saloon. BR Wagon Lot No. 3379. Swindon 1960. B4 bogies.

999508	**SO**	RK	*SO*	ZA

High Speed Track Recording Coach. Can either be locomotive hauled (accompanied by 977335/7/8) or included between DMU vehicles 977391/2. Purpose built Mark 2. B4 bogies.

999550	**RK**	RK	*SO*	ZA

TEST TRAIN BRAKE FORCE RUNNERS

These vehicles are included in test trains to provide brake force. Those listed are numbered in the former BR departmental number series and are not used for any other purposes. Other vehicles included in this book may also be similarly used on a temporary basis if required. Converted from BR Mark 1 BSK, RKB, RB, RU, FOs and BR Mark 2 TSO, SO, FK, BFKs.

975051. Lot No. 30025 Wolverton 1950–52. B4 bogies.
977084. Lot No. 30514 Cravens 1958–61. B5 bogies.
977085. Lot No. 30633 Swindon 1959–62. Commonwealth bogies.
977193. Lot No. 30632 Swindon 1959–61. Commonwealth bogies.
977331. Lot No. 30721 Swindon 1961–63. Commonwealth bogies.
977387/468/70/773/801/2. Lot No. 30751 Derby 1964–7. B4 bogies.
977388. Lot No. 30242 Doncaster 1955–56. B4 bogies.
977389. Lot No. 30091 Doncaster 1953–54. B4 bogies.
977390/546. Lot No. 30810 Derby 1969–70. B4 bogies.
977449/50/594. Lot No. 30472 BRCW 1957–59. B4 bogies.
977595. Lot No. 30825 Derby 1969–72. B4 bogies.
977788/94/5. Lot No. 30823 Derby 1969–72. B4 bogies.
977789. Lot No. 30837 Derby 1971–72. B4 bogies.
977790/1/2/6. Lot No. 30844 Derby 1972–73. B4 bogies.
977793. Lot No. 30795 Derby 1969–70. B4 bogies.
977905. Lot No. 30573 GRCW 1959–60. B4 bogies.

Non-Standard Livery: 977387 is BR blue and grey lined out in white with a red stripe. 977773 is blue and grey with a cream stripe. 977788-94 are Adtranz White with yellow stripe.

975051	(34133)	**B**	E		CW
977084	(1505)	**B**	E		CW
977085	(336, 1637)	**B**	E		CW
977193	(1989)	**B**	E		CW
977331	(35444)	**BG**	AM		ZH
977387	(5195)	**0**	SO		ZA
977388	(3071)	**BG**	AM		ZH
977389	(3049)	**BG**	AM		ZH
977390	(3164, 6410)	**B**	E		CW
977449	(3086)	**B**	E		CW
977450	(3087)	**B**	E		CW
977468	(5169)	**SO**	SO	*SO*	ZA
977470	(5134)	**SO**	SO	*SO*	ZA
977546	(3165, 6416)	**BG**	RC		ZH
977594	(3093)	**BG**	RC		ZH
977595	(13573)	**BG**	E		CW
977773	(5182)	**0**	AM		ZA
977788	(17157)	**0**	BT	*E*	ZF
977789	(5765)	**0**	BT	*E*	ZF
977790	(5830)	**0**	BT	*E*	ZF
977791	(5855)	**0**	BT	*E*	ZF
977792	(5856)	**0**	BT	*E*	ZF

977793	(5596)	**0**	BT	*E*	ZF
977794	(17139)	**0**	BT	*E*	ZF
977795	(17162)	**BG**	EM		ZH
977796	(5898)	**BG**	EM		ZH
977801	(5153)	**SO**	RK	*SO*	ZA
977802	(5176)	**SO**	RK	*SO*	ZA
977905	(35292, 80215)	**SO**	SO	*SO*	ZA

BREAKDOWN TRAIN COACHES

These coaches are formed in trains used for the recovery of derailed railway vehicles and were converted from BR Mark 1 BCK, BG, BSK and SK . They are numbered in the former BR departmental number series. The current use of each vehicle is given. 975611–613 were previously converted to trailer luggage vans in 1968. BR Mark 1 bogies.

Non-standard livery: All vehicles are yellow.

975080. Lot No. 30155 Wolverton 1955–56.
975087. Lot No. 30032 Wolverton 1951–52.
975463/573. Lot No. 30156 Wolverton 1954–55.
975465/477/494. Lot No. 30233 GRCW 1955–57.
975471. Lot No. 30095 Wolverton 1953–55.
975481/482/484/574. Lot No. 30141 GRCW 1954–55.
975498. Lot No. 30074 Wolverton 1953–54.
975611–613. Lot No. 30162 Pressed Steel 1954–57.
975639, 977088/235. Lot No. 30229 Metro-Cammell 1955–57.
977095/107. Lot No. 30425 Metro-Cammell 1956–58.

975080	(25079)	r	**0**	RK	*E*	TO	Tool Van
975087	(34289)	r	**0**	RK	*E*	CD	Generator Van
975463	(34721)	r	**0**	RK	*E*	TE	Staff Coach
975465	(35109)	r	**0**	RK	*E*	TO	Staff Coach
975471	(34543)	r	**0**	RK	*E*	CD	Staff & Tool Coach
975477	(34108)	r	**0**	RK	*E*	CD	Staff Coach
975481	(34606)	r	**0**	RK	*E*	TO	Generator Van
975482	(34602)	r	**0**	RK	*E*	TE	Generator Van
975484	(34591)		**0**	DR		CS	Generator Van
975494	(35082)	r	**0**	RK	*E*	CF	Generator Van
975498	(34637)	r	**0**	RK	*E*	TE	Tool Van
975573	(34729)	r	**0**	RK	*E*	CF	Staff Coach
975574	(34599)	r	**0**	RK	*E*	OC	Staff Coach
975611	(80915, 68201)	r	**0**	RK	*E*	OC	Generator Van
975612	(80922, 68203)	r	**0**	RK	*E*	CF	Tool Van
975613	(80918, 68202)	r	**0**	RK	*E*	OC	Tool Van
975639	(35016)		**0**	DR		CS	Tool Van
977088	(34990)		**0**	RK	*E*	CD	Generator Van
977095	(21210)		**0**	DR		CS	Staff Coach
977107	(21202)		**0**	RK	*E*	CD	Staff Coach
977235	(34989)		**0**	RK	*E*	CD	Tool Van

9. NPCCS AWAITING DISPOSAL

This list contains the last known locations of NPCCS vehicles awaiting disposal. The definition of which vehicles are "awaiting disposal" is somewhat vague, but generally speaking these are vehicles of types not now in normal service or vehicles which have been damaged by fire, vandalism or collision.

80330	Bristol Pylle Hill
80336	Bristol East Yard
80338	Bristol East Yard
80735	Perth Holding Sidings
80865	Hornsey Sand Terminal
84197	Worksop
84364	Doncaster West Yard
84519	Crewe South Yard
92198	ZB
92562	OM
93180	Derby South Dock Siding
93234	Hayes & Harlington
93358	Mossend Yard
93446	Crewe South Yard
93457	Cricklewood Rubbish Terminal
93482	Bedford Civil Engineers Sidings
93542	Hayes & Harlington
93579	DY
93723	Bletchley T&RSMD
93930	Crewe South Yard
95366	Bristol East Yard
96177	CP
99648	Eastleigh East Yard
395762	Margam Yard
975454	TO
975462	Three Bridges WRD
975491	TO
975991	Crewe South Yard
977144	PY
977182	Eastleigh Down CS
977183	Eastleigh Down CS
977359	ZN
977399	NL
977510	FP
977726	Wavertree Yard, Liverpool
977781	DY
977782	DY
977783	DY
977784	DY
977908	NC
977914	DY
977916	DY

10. CODES USED IN THIS BOOK

LIVERY CODES

Coaching stock vehicles are in Intercity (light grey/red stripe/white stripe/dark grey) livery unless otherwise indicated. The colour of the lower half of the bodyside is stated first.

AE	AEA Technology Rail (dark blue with white stripe)
AR	Anglia Railways (turquoise blue with white stripe)
B	BR blue.
BG	BR blue & grey lined out in white.
CC	BR carmine & cream lined out in black & gold ('blood & custard').
CH	BR Western Region/GWR chocolate & cream.
CS	Scotrail Caledonian sleepers. Two tone purple with silver stripe.
DR	Direct Rail Services. Dark blue with light blue roof.
DS	Danske Statsbaner (Danish State Railways), Blue and red with moon and star motifs.
E	English Welsh & Scottish Railway (Maroon with gold stripe).
EP	European Passenger Services (Two-tone grey with dark blue roof).
FG	First Great Western (green and ivory with thin green and broad gold stripes).
FW	First Great Western (Indigo blue with white roof and gold, pink and white stripes)
G	BR Southern Region Green.
GN	Great North Eastern Railway (dark blue with an orange bodyside stripe and gold or silver GNER lettering).
HB	HSBC Rail (Oxford blue & white).
LN	LNER Tourist green & cream.
M	BR Maroon, generally lined out in straw and black.
MM	Midland Mainline (grey and green with three orange bodyside stripes.
MS	Merseyrail Departmental (dark grey and yellow with Merseyrail logo).
N	Network SouthEast (grey/white/red/white/blue/white).
NB	Network SouthEast livery with the red stripe repainted blue.
0	Non standard livery (see notes in class headings for details).
P	Porterbrook Leasing (purple and grey).
PC	Pullman Car Company (umber and cream with gold lettering).
R	Plain Red.
RB	Riviera Trains (Oxford blue & cream, lined out in gold).
RK	Railtrack (green & blue).
RM	Royal Mail. Red with Yellow stripes above solebar.
RP	Royal Train. Claret, lined out in red and black).
RR	Regional Railways (grey/light blue/white/dark blue).
RX	Rail express systems (dark grey and red with or without blue markings).
RY	BR parcels sector. Red with yellow stripes above solebar.
SO	Serco Railtest (red & grey).
V	Virgin Trains (red with black doors extending into bodysides, three white lower bodysides stripes).
VN	Venice Simplon Orient Express 'Northern Belle' *(Crimson lake and cream).*
WR	Waterman Railways (maroon with cream stripes).
WV	Waterman Railways VIP (West Coast Joint Stock lined purple lake).

OWNER CODES

14	75014 Locomotive Operators Group
24	6024 Preservation Society
62	Princess Royal Locomotive Trust
A	Angel Train Contracts
AE	AEA Technology Rail
AM	Alstom UK
AR	Anglia Railways
BK	Scottish Railway Preservation Society
BT	Bombardier Transportation
CW	Cotswold Rail Engineering
DR	Direct Rail Services
E	English Welsh & Scottish Railway
ER	Eastleigh Railway Preservation Society
EU	Eurostar (UK)
FR	Fragonset Railways
FS	Flying Scotsman Railways
GS	The Great Scottish & Western Railway Company
GW	First Great Western
H	HSBC Rail. (formerly Forward Trust Rail)
IE	Ian Storey Engineering
LW	London & North Western Railway Company
MH	Mid-Hants Railway
MN	Merchant Navy Locomotive Preservation Society
NE	North Eastern Locomotive Preservation Group
NR	National Railway Museum
NY	North Yorkshire Moors Railway
P	Porterbrook Leasing Company
RA	Railfilms
RK	Railtrack
RS	Rail Charter Services
RV	Riviera Trains
SA	Sea Containers Rail Services
SH	Scottish Highland Railway Company
SO	Serco Railtest
SV	Severn Valley Railway
VS	Venice Simplon Orient Express
VT	Vintage Trains
WC	West Coast Railway Company
WT	Wessex Trains

OPERATION CODES

The two letter operating codes give the use to which the vehicle is at present put. For vehicles in regular use, this is the code for the train operating company For other vehicles the actual type of use is shown. If no operating code is shown then the vehicle is not at present in use.

A	Angel Trains Contracts
AE	AEA Technology Rail
AR	Anglia Railways
DR	Direct Rail Services
E	English Welsh & Scottish Railway
EU	Eurostar (UK)
GN	Great North Eastern Railway
GW	First Great Western
H	HSBC Rail
MM	Midland Mainline
OS	Locomotive support coach
P	Porterbrook Leasing Company.
RK	Railtrack
RP	Royal Train
SO	Serco Railtest
SR	ScotRail
SS	Used normally on special or charter passenger services
VL	Wales & Borders Valley Lines business unit
VW	Virgin West Coast
VX	Virgin Cross Country

DEPOT, WORKS & LOCATION CODES

Code	*Depot*	*Operator*
BD	Birkenhead North T&RSMD	Arriva Trains Merseyside
BK	Barton Hill T&RSMD (Bristol)	EWS
BN	Bounds Green T&RSMD (London)	GNER
BQ	Bury (Greater Manchester)	East Lancashire Railway
BT	Bo'ness (West Lothian)	Bo'ness & Kinneil Railway
CD	Crewe Diesel TMD	EWS
CF	Cardiff Canton T&RSMD	Wales & Borders Trains
CJ	Clapham Yard CSD (London)	South West Trains
CL	Carlisle Upperby (closed)	*Storage location only*
CO	Cranmore (Somerset)	East Somerset Railway
CP	Crewe Carriage T&RSMD	London & North Western Railway Co.
CQ	The Railway Age (Crewe)	London & North Western Railway Co.
CS	Carnforth T&RSMD	West Coast Railway Company
CU*	Carlisle Currock	EWS
CW	Crewe South Yard	*Storage location only*
DI	Didcot Railway Centre	Great Western Society
DY	Derby Etches Park T&RSMD	Maintrain
EC	Craigentinny T&RSMD (Edinburgh)	GNER
EN	Euston Downside CARMD (London)	EWS
FP	Ferme Park CSD	GNER
HE	Hornsey T&RSMD	West Anglia Great Northern
HT	Heaton T&RSMD	Arriva Trains Northern
HY*	Hinksey Yard (Oxford)	*Storage location only*
IL	Ilford T&RSMD	First Great Eastern
IS	Inverness CARMD	Scotrail
KM	Carlisle Kingmoor TMD	Direct Rail Services

KR	Kidderminster	Severn Valley Railway
KT	MoD Kineton DM (Warwickshire)	MoD Defence Rail Group
LA	Laira T&RSMD (Plymouth)	First Great Western
LT*	MoD Longtown DM (Cumbria)	MoD Defence Rail Group
MA	Manchester Longsight CARMD	West Coast Traincare
MB	MoD DSDA Bicester	MoD Defence Rail Group
ML	Motherwell TMD	EWS
MM	Fire Service College, Moreton-in-Marsh	*Storage location only*
NC	Norwich Crown Point T&RSMD	Anglia Railways
NL	Neville Hill IC T&RSMD (Leeds)	Maintrain
NP	North Pole International (London)	Eurostar (UK)
NY	Grosmont (North Yorkshire)	North Yorkshire Moors Railway
OC	Old Oak Common CARMD (London)	EWS
OM	Old Oak Common CARMD (London)	First Great Western
OO	Old Oak Common HSTMD (London)	First Great Western
OY	Oxley T&RSMD (Wolverhampton)	West Coast Traincare
PC	Polmadie T&RSMD (Glasgow)	West Coast Traincare
PM	St. Phillips Marsh T&RSMD (Bristol)	First Great Western
PY*	MoD DERA Shoeburyness	MoD Defence Rail Group
PZ	Penzance CARMD	First Great Western
RL	Ropley	Mid-Hants Railway
SK	Swanwick Junction (Derbyshire)	Midland Railway Centre
SL	Stewarts Lane T&RSMD (London)	Gatwick Express
SZ	Southall (Greater London)	Flying Scotsman Railways
TE	Thornaby TMD	EWS
TM	Tyseley Locomotive Works	Birmingham Railway Museum
TO	Toton TMD	EWS
TS	Tyseley T&RSMD (Birmingham)	Maintrain
YK	National Railway Museum (York)	Science Museum
ZA	Railway Technical Centre (Derby)	Serco, AEA Technology
ZB	Wabtec Doncaster	Wabtec
ZC	Crewe Works	Bombardier Transportation
ZD	Derby, Litchurch Lane Works	Bombardier Transportation
ZF	Doncaster Works	Bombardier Transportation
ZG	Eastleigh Works	Alstom UK
ZH	Springburn Works (Glasgow)	Alstom UK
ZN	Wolverton Works	Alstom UK

* Unofficial code

ABBREVIATIONS

CARMD	Carriage Maintenance Depot
CSD	Carriage Servicing Depot
DERA	Defence Evaluation & Research Agency
DM	Defence Munitions
DSDA	Defence Distribution and Agency
MoD	Ministry of Defence
TMD	Traction Maintenance Depot
T&RSMD	Traction and Rolling Stock Maintenance Depot